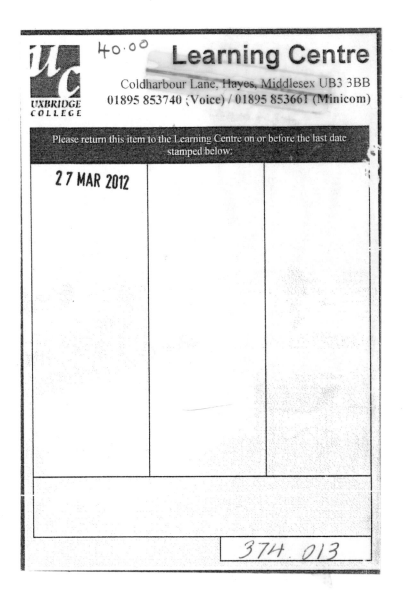

40.00

Learning Centre

Coldharbour Lane, Hayes, Middlesex UB3 3BB
01895 853740 (Voice) / 01895 853661 (Minicom)

Quality Improvement

in Adult Vocational Education and Training

Transforming Skills for
the Global Economy

Nicky Perry & David Sherlock

**KOGAN
PAGE**

London and Philadelphia

Publisher's note

Every possible effort has been made to ensure that the information contained in this book is accurate at the time of going to press, and the publisher and authors cannot accept responsibility for any errors or omissions, however caused. No responsibility for loss or damage occasioned to any person acting, or refraining from action, as a result of the material in this publication can be accepted by the publisher or any of the authors.

First published in Great Britain and the United States in 2008 by Kogan Page Limited

120 Pentonville Road
London N1 9JN
United Kingdom
www.koganpage.com

525 South 4th Street, #241
Philadelphia PA 19147
USA

ISBN   978 0 7494 5103 5

British Library Cataloguing-in-Publication Data

A CIP record for this book is available from the British Library.

Library of Congress Cataloging-in-Publication Data

Sherlock, David.
  Quality improvement in adult vocational education and training : transforming skills for the global economy / David Sherlock and Nicky Perry.
      p. cm.
  Includes index.
  ISBN 978-0-7494-5103-5
1. Employer-supported education. 2. Career education. 3. Technical education. 4. Occupational training. 5. Employees–Training of. 6. Vocational education. I. Perry, Nick, 1942– II. Title.
  HF5549.5.T7S53 2008
  374'.013--dc22

                                                    2007047480

Typeset by Saxon Graphics Ltd, Derby
Printed and bound in India by Replika Press Pvt Ltd

To our families;
left behind too often when we were
on the road learning our trade.

Contents

Foreword – David Blunkett   *viii*

Acknowledgements   *x*

Introduction   **1**

1 Why change: the challenges of globalization   **8**
Globalization 10; The British experience 11;
The role of skills and productivity 15; National skills
strategies 19; Technical and vocational education and
training (TVET) 20; Case Study 1 – Unipart plc 26

2 Standards and frameworks   **29**
Shaping a judgement 32; What is good learning? 34;
A new framework 35; What is evidence? 39; And why? 42;
Case Study 2 – BMW Group UK Ltd 43

3 Using the Framework   **46**
The value of qualifications 48; Measuring added value 50;
Effective learning 53; Equality and diversity 55;
Matching learning to learners 56; Support for learning 59;
Assessing leadership 61; Grading 63; Case Study 3 – West
Berkshire Adult Community Learning 64

4   How to judge learning   **67**
It helps to be watched 69; Preparing to shine 71;
What does good learning look like? 75; Making observation
credible 78; Giving the messages 82; Case Study 4 –
Feedback 86

5   Using self-assessment   **88**
Twins 90; Loving self-assessment 91; Getting it done 95;
Data, data, data 98; Self-assessing what? 100; A self-critical
culture 102; Case Study 5 – JHP Training 104

6   Using data   **107**
Cooking the books 108; Seeing is believing 110;
Getting behind the numbers 111; A focus on outcome 113;
Comparing similar things 114; An example in detail 117;
Case Study 6 – Toni & Guy 120

7   Consequences   **123**
Driving home change 124; Confirming progress 126;
The helping hand 128; Defining the PDU offering 131;
The legacy 133; Case Study 7 – Cheadle Royal Industries 135;
Case Study 8 – Learning and skills in prisons 137

8   Building a national quality movement   **139**
Why *Excalibur* worked 143; Accumulating corporate
memory 146; Instructional materials 147; Face-to-face
teaching 150; Good practice online 151; The Quality
Champions Programme 154; Masters of quality
assessment 155; Case Study 9 – Military training 156

9   Persuading   **158**
Walking the walk 159; Defining the destination 164;
The medium for the message 168; The language of
aspiration 171; Case Study 10 – *Vive la différence* 173

10 Proving it **176**

Case Study 11 – A fair cop 187

11 Adapting the model **190**

A new pattern in England 194; Uprating an organization 199;
A different culture 201; Reflection 203; Case Study 12 – Jamie
Oliver and *Fifteen* 204

Index *207*

Foreword

I warmly welcome this timely new book by David Sherlock and Nicky Perry. It vividly describes what they learnt and what they did to transform the quality of vocational education and training. It shows how England's experience can benefit people coming to terms with the open global economy, worldwide.

Vocational approaches to learning are still far too often seen as second best. The same could be said of learning during adult life. When I took up my job as Secretary of State for Education and Employment as a member of a government determined to bring new levels of success and prosperity to our country, I was sure this neglect had to end. Our economy depends as much, if not more, on the skills of people at work now and in keeping those people at the cutting edge throughout their lives, as it does on bringing through new generations of able young people.

In my Foreword to my policy paper, *The Learning Age*, I said that turning things round depended not only on raising dramatically the quality of teaching and learning, but also on fostering our people's joy in learning. Success in the globalized world rests on practical skill but also on building a civilised society, full of creativity and at ease with itself.

I was proud to launch both the Training Standards Council and later the Adult Learning Inspectorate with David in charge and Nicky leading on inspection quality. My direction to David was to report publicly and to me without fear or favour. Improving the quality of teaching and learning, fast and for everybody, is not always a gentle business. The stakes are high. There are always vested interests standing in the way of progress. The stark truth, as David and his team found it and told it, was often a matter for deep anxiety in the early days. If I brought something special to putting things right, it was a sense of outrage that so much training for work was so bad.

I well remember sending tremors through my government department when it became clear that the quality of training for carers of our old people was the worst of all. How could we be at ease with that?

What David, Nicky and their team did was to change inspection from only a means of making judgements about the quality of learning into a way of promptly making it better. They found ways to persuade, to convince, to recruit the people they inspected into enthusiastically working towards being world class. In my long career in public life, I can think of few, if any, public agencies which managed simultaneously to be so tough and uncompromising in the demands they made, and so well-liked and strongly supported by the colleges, companies and charities they worked with, as did the Adult Learning Inspectorate.

One last point before you get into the book. The tone is human and warm. That truly reflects the people involved and their organizations. That is not coincidental to the success they achieved. If I wrote about the joy and creativity of learning when I started out in government, they made sure those same things were felt and lived in adult learning.

This is an important book. It should help make everyone confident enough to try what the very best colleges, companies and charities already can do. It shows how widely scattered networks of independent organizations can be motivated to work together. As we in England move towards a system with greater provider ownership and self-regulation, it sets out clearly the fundamentals that have to be mastered to drive up quality in any form of technical and vocational education and training. It encourages our friends in other countries to profit from this country's successes and failures.

David and Nicky are right that the open global market can bring prosperity more quickly and to more people than anything we have known before. Here are some practical ways to make that happen.

Rt Hon David Blunkett MP

Acknowledgements

We would not have dreamt of writing this book without the experience of inspection. We have learnt what we know by working with great colleagues in the Further Education Funding Council (FEFC), the Training Standards Council and the Adult Learning Inspectorate (ALI). Among them we should mention Sir William Stubbs and Terry Melia of the FEFC, doyen among chief inspectors, from whom we learnt our trade. Lisa Yeoman, Coral Newton, Keith Marshall, Denis McEnhill and Andrew Tyley worked with us to set up and run the Training Standards Council and the ALI, as did our 20 original inspectors, many of whom stayed throughout and achieved senior positions. We should mention particularly Lesley Davies and John Landeryou, formerly assistant directors of the ALI. The success of the Provider Development Unit owed much to the leadership of Pat Hornsby and that of *Excalibur* to William Lewis and Ian Smith. Public life in England owes much to the many people who give their time unpaid to be members of boards. To those who contributed to the Training Standards Council and the ALI and became friends as well as colleagues, we offer our thanks. To everyone we have worked with closely in inspection for the past 14 years, we owe our affection and gratitude.

There were political leaders who influenced matters at decisive moments. Principal among them has been David Blunkett MP who, as Secretary of State for Education and Employment, was man-midwife to both the Training Standards Council and the ALI. David's passionate concern and determination to make things change when alerted to bad training or unfairness kept everyone on their toes. We are grateful for his generous Foreword. Mention should also be made of Margaret Hodge MP to whom belongs the honour of demanding that the ALI's Provider Development Unit should come into being, and of Adam Ingram JP MP, former Minister for the Armed Forces, a good man to work with when the going gets tough.

Our work was funded overwhelmingly by public money in the care of civil servants. Peerless among them was Bas Norriss who almost shared our decade with the Training Standards Council and the ALI and eased the path of two restlessly innovative organizations through thickets often obstructive to the unfamiliar. Supportive too, particularly in the early days when we had yet to prove our worth, were Nick Stuart, John Hedger, Sir Leigh Lewis, Suzanne Orr, Peter Lauener, Clive Mitchell and Simon Baddeley. We thank them for their confidence in us and their forbearance.

The opportunity to test our ideas with overseas governments has most often been supported by the British Council. Our thanks are due particularly to Ruth Gee, Katie Epstein and Tony Calderbank who have championed the cause of technical and vocational education and training (TVET).

We have learnt a great deal from our fellow toilers in the English public service, tossing ideas and experiences back and forth to what we hope was mutual benefit. Prominent among its leaders have been Chris Humphries, Alan Tuckett, Chris Hughes, Lynne Sedgmore, Dame Ruth Silver, Ioan Morgan, Graham Hoyle and Ken Boston, creators of the zeitgeist of quality in adult learning. Influential on us, too, have been Rear Admiral Simon Goodall and Commodore Tony Miklinski, formerly of the Royal Navy; Phil Wheatley, head of the Prison Service, and his predecessor, Martin Narey; Lord David Ramsbotham and Ann Owers, successive chief inspectors of prisons; and Robin Field-Smith of Her Majesty's Inspectorate of Constabulary.

Most of all, we have benefited from enthusiastically sharing the goals of colleges and training providers in England. Even their leaders are too numerous to mention. They have been our inspiration and it is their success that should encourage everyone who reads this book. We are particularly grateful to those who have given permission for their organizations to be described in the case studies.

Our warm thanks are due to Suzy Powling who forced us to refine the concept of this book and persuaded us that the labour of writing it was survivable; to Elizabeth Graney who has streamlined what she describes as Sherlock's 'baroque' prose over the years; and Lynda Holcroft who transformed some vile manuscript into material fit for our publisher. At Kogan Page, our thanks are due to our original commissioning editor Charlotte Atyeo, to chief executive Helen Kogan, to Hannah Berry, our current editor, and to Helen Savill, project editor for this book.

David Sherlock and Nicky Perry

Introduction

Introductions are seldom read, but we hope this one might be an exception.

Quality Improvement in Adult Vocational Education and Training shows how the quality of skills training for adults can be improved dramatically – and quickly. Finding a way to do this is a priority for the world's governments today as they strive for success in the global economy. Our starting point is a quality assessment technique particular to the United Kingdom, inspection, and in this Introduction we chart how, over time and with experience, this was transformed into an element of a universally relevant quality improvement model. Many countries have deep-seated reservations about the concept of 'inspection' but by adapting some of its techniques, and adding others from the worlds of modern business and communications, a uniquely potent engine for changing behaviour and culture in learning can be created.

Inspection in the United Kingdom has a long history. It began with schools inspectors in the 1830s, helping to guarantee consistent standards in the new public education service. Among their number was the poet and critic Matthew Arnold, son of Thomas Arnold, the fabled reforming headmaster who appears in the novel *Tom Brown's Schooldays*. He, among others less celebrated, set the tone for their new profession. Arnold's approach was that of the humanist, supporting teachers wherever he could in a job he recognized as extraordinarily difficult. Something of the same philosophy spread through other inspectorates created to regulate each facet of Britain's industrial revolution: railways, factories, public health and much more besides. The intention was to learn from shortcomings – even disasters and accidents – in order to stimulate improvement. This was an agenda which cast the inspector as a figure independent of the government of the day; the citizen's expert representative and advocate. Inspection became an accepted and respected part of British civil society.

It was a club we were happy to join. But when we did so in 1993, colder winds were blowing around inspection, from the realization by the British government that the country was falling behind its peers in the Organization for Economic Co-operation & Development (OECD). Schools, and the examination performance of children in them, were too often inadequate. The consequence was the break-up of Her Majesty's Inspectorate, with its direct lineage from Arnold. In its stead were introduced three specialist bodies: the Office for Standards in Education (Ofsted); the inspectorate of the Further Education Funding Council (FEFC); and the Quality Assurance Agency for Higher Education (QAA). They were charged with the independent quality assurance of schools, further education colleges and universities, respectively.

With these new organizations came new practices in inspection. Radical at the time, they greatly increased its potential effectiveness. Among them were the introduction of a fixed inspection cycle, with every institution inspected every four years or so; prompt re-inspection of those found wanting, with the prospect of severe sanctions for a second failure; a requirement for regular self-assessment by every institution; the introduction of numerical grades to summarize performance in every significant area of activity, including corporate management; and publication of inspection reports. This new regime mainly affected publicly owned institutions, and it was given statutory force. A poor inspection result could and did lead to the sacking of senior managers and the closure or enforced merger of institutions.

This brisk treatment was most evident in schools, where the new inspection methods coincided with the introduction of a highly prescriptive national curriculum and a weakening of the role traditionally taken by local government. The school, its governing body and its principal were left to manage the budget, deliver national objectives and sink or swim according to their success in meeting national targets. In these circumstances, Ofsted's focus was logically inevitable: inspectors concentrated on the performance of individual teachers, observed in the classroom. This focus brought forth a new phrase in educational debate: 'name and shame'. Name and shame severed the supportive tradition of Arnold. It heralded a new abrasiveness, a loss of trust in educators' professionalism and a faith in parent or customer power to punish laggards through market forces.

Tough regulation of publicly funded learning became the favoured norm. Where one of its agencies was believed to be failing in exercising sufficient control, government quickly lost confidence in it. The FEFC was closed in 2001, following a series of financial scandals in colleges, despite its protestations that the limitations of its legal powers had not allowed it to intervene. The potential for increasing the influence of central government through inspection, even to areas where modest government subsidies partly funded learning alongside money from employers or learners themselves, was also realized. In 1997, this led to the foundation of the Training Standards Council inspectorate. We resigned from the FEFC to establish this. It was, in many respects, a critical moment. About £1 billion a year was being passed by central government through 72 local training and enterprise councils in England and Wales to an indeterminate number of private and charitable providers of training. The most common award available through work-based training was the relatively new National Vocational Qualification (NVQ). Its guiding philosophy was that competency in workplace skills could be judged through observed performance of a series of tightly defined tasks. This austere approach set aside any notion of how *well* someone might be able to do a job and the notion of pride in fine workmanship or excellence. The credibility of the NVQ was sinking fast; its initials were held to stand for 'not very qualified'. And there was a prevailing atmosphere that all private training providers were probably using suspect financial practices and anything we could do to catch them out would be welcomed.

Fortunately, the reality was rather different. It turned out that there were between 1,500 and 2,000 training providers, the more extravagant estimates of up to 10,000 having been based on confusion between main contractors and a variety of subcontractors offering everything from assessment to work experience. We were interested only in holding to account the main contractors for everything done in their name. It also turned out that many of the principles inherited from our experience with the FEFC – transparency, openness, an attempt to work *with* the organization being inspected rather than doing unpleasant things *to* it – were adaptable to our new circumstances. To these principles was added a new one: that quality should be judged by the level of benefit that training brought to each learner. This turned out to be a seminal decision. On one level, this benchmark was one with which few could possibly disagree. More profoundly, it opened up more sophisticated avenues of inspection. Where our inspectors found reason to criticize management practices, for example, they had to justify themselves not in terms of their personal hobby-horses about management but by citing evidence of ill-effects on learners. 'Data management is poor', they might say 'and this is a problem because learners are unaware of the progress they are making and are qualifying far too slowly as a result.'

We insisted that all our inspectors should be occupational specialists. Only engineers would inspect engineering, for example, and only hairdressers hairdressing. We produced the first framework guiding both self-assessment and inspection in one unstuffy handbook, demonstrating that we had no hidden agenda. We reclassified the arcane Standard Occupational Code, which listed thousands of jobs, into 14 'areas of learning', allowing us to make comparisons between topics of broadly similar character and importance. We introduced electronic publishing to the world of British inspection so that reports on training appeared on the internet. And we fostered a business-like culture. The Training Standards Council had no statutory powers but undertook its inspections as a condition of every contract involving government money. It was a company, subject to most of the same disciplines as its customers.

It worked. A sense of identity and even empathy with training providers prompted honest dialogue without diminishing the rigour of the judgements made and published. In our four-year existence, we added to our portfolio the inspection of welfare-to-work programmes for unemployed people and occupational training in prisons. This was a regime that made clear for all to see that most employers and private training providers cared as much for their trainees as their public sector counterparts.

The success of the Training Standards Council and a troubled existence for the FEFC in the years after we had left it combined to give us the opportunity to found and lead a new body, the Adult Learning Inspectorate (ALI), from the autumn of 2000. The ALI gathered together the work of the FEFC and the TSC and added to it: adult and community learning from Ofsted; new publicly subsidized learning provision, notably a national e-learning network; and, through authority to undertake inspection on a commissioned basis, quality assessment in some wholly untrodden fields, including the police, the armed services and overseas, notably in the Middle East.

The ALI watched over the birth of a new political construct: the learning and skills sector. This was to consist of all work-based learning for people over the age of 16: all college-based learning for people over the age of 18 (some 80 per cent of all further education students); all adult learning other than degrees and similar higher education awards. Where inspection responsibilities abutted, as they did with Ofsted in further education colleges, the ALI worked in partnership with others. In all, the ALI had responsibility for guaranteeing the quality of learning for some 5 million people. The public, private and not-for-profit organizations involved ranged from colleges to local authorities to multinational employers to small specialist training companies to major charities serving disadvantaged or disabled people. One week an ALI inspector might be working in a century-old academic institution; the next in a high-security prison; and the next in a company making products famous the world over. The ALI had to help create a sense of identity and shared ambition and we did it, first, through launching a monthly newspaper called *Talisman*.

The ALI was to be the mature expression of our approach to inspection. It consolidated our insistence on inspection solely by professional specialists; on a single public framework shaping both self-assessment and inspection judgements; on reaching evidence-based judgements through open debate with the participation of a senior representative of the organization being inspected; on prompt, candid, graded publication of our findings on the internet; on benefit to the individual learner as the principal criterion for determining quality.

Equally, we had become convinced through experience that traditional approaches to inspection – collect evidence, pronounce judgement and walk away – were inadequate. Not only was progress achieved in that way painfully slow but the atmosphere created by hawkish application of regulatory inspection was often highly confrontational. What might be tolerable – just – in state-owned provision was certainly counterproductive on privately owned premises where the government subsidy for training might well be a negligible fraction of the company's income stream. Bluntly, unless inspection clearly added value in terms significant to the organization being inspected, any idea of a learning and skills sector – a public service delivered by organizations in a wide range of ownership – would be blown away.

Our solution was to offer quality improvement services. Quality improvement was the clearly defined end towards which quality assessment – inspection – was a necessary step. The ALI's quality improvement services consisted of a rescue-service for weak providers, the Provider Development Unit and a wider quality enhancement network, online as well as face to face, called *Excalibur*. In essence, we had brought inspection from its root in public regulation to a point where it could stand alongside other major modern approaches to quality improvement. The ALI tied together aspiration, assessment and support for improvement.

The position of the inspector is, as it has been since Arnold's day, one of privilege. Inspectors have privileged access to premises and information. They have the privilege of observing other professionals going about their work and of asking them very direct questions to which a full answer is expected. They have the privilege of spending time with teachers and learners, collecting evidence and building judgements from it. They have the privilege of publishing those judgements, without redress when they cause harm unless the inspection was negligent or malicious.

Our stance is that these privileges have to be paid for by using the knowledge gained to benefit learning providers and learners directly. We have found sympathy for that position, and interest in adopting and adapting it to meet local needs, in many organizations outside the British publicly funded training system and in a number of countries beyond the United Kingdom. The ALI fulfilled commissioned inspections to a value of over £1 million a year from when it began offering the service and could have done much more. We have described and sometimes applied our approach in many countries, including Australia, Bahrain, Canada, Oman, Saudi Arabia, Vietnam and Yemen.

This book is our return for the privileges we have received as inspectors. It codifies our ideas and relates them to the acute challenge to raise productivity – national, organizational and individual – which faces every country seeking prosperity in an open, global market. There is no intrinsic reason why the United Kingdom, a small island on the edge of Europe with a large population and few natural resources, should be the world's fifth-largest economy. Prime Minister Margaret Thatcher, when she presided over the transformation of Britain into one of the world's first knowledge-based economies, convinced the British that the world did not owe us a living. We know that if the creativity and energy of its people falter, then this country will sink into obscurity. We *have* to achieve improvements in the skills, capability and engagement of all our people. We *have* to succeed.

We believe that our experience of inspection in Britain, crystallized in our work with the ALI, offers clues to help answer the question everyone seeking such improvement first asks: 'Where do I start?' We are not saying to others that they should do what we have done. Rather, we offer ourselves as guides to anyone bold enough to innovate and experiment: the British experience offers a laboratory in which much can be learnt.

1

Why change: the challenges of globalization

Let us start by taking you to an unfamiliar place. We are in Yemen. It is 2007 and we are running a quality improvement workshop at the Sana'a Community College. The delegates come from all over the Arabic-speaking world; half of them are Yemenis who work in colleges and technical training centres throughout the country. Everyone's aim is clear. It is to learn how to raise the performance of technical and vocational teaching so that it can help people escape poverty.

Why Yemen? It is the only developing country in the Gulf region. The issues are stark here. You can see them spelt out by the beggars and the ancient, battered cars on the street. You can see them in the contrast between energetic, ambitious women and many of their menfolk, who spend every afternoon of life with one cheek bulging with the local narcotic of choice, Qat. Like the coca leaf of the Andes, Qat soothes the daily struggle. You can see them in the glorious architectural heritage from pre-Islamic times as well as Islamic, proudly shown to you by self-appointed child guides. It is just beginning to attract tourists enterprising enough not to be deterred by the litter of plastic bags left over from yesterday's Qat and the official warnings of kidnap and violence against westerners. You can see them in the small beginnings of an oil industry, a half-century behind the rest of the Gulf because of earlier misrule and mayhem. You can see them everywhere in human and material potential yet to be fulfilled. The most cheerful, hard-working country in the Middle East, with the most fertile land and the richest and most visible history, waiting for the spark to bring prosperity.

Like everywhere else we have ever worked, there was no shortage of people to say 'We cannot do anything. The system gets in the way. It is the ministry's fault; the college's fault; employers' fault; management's fault.' And as we have sometimes done before, we told them a story. It was 1977. David Sherlock had been asked to go and give technical advice to Bangladesh, not only newly formed as an independent nation after a brutal conflict with Pakistan, but devastated too by floods. Every night's television news showed millions of the displaced and starving in refugee camps, cared for by a few heroic foreign nurses and willing local volunteers. Before leaving, he went to seek the advice of an old hand in third-world development, who asked 'How do you feel?' 'Terrified. I'm not sure how much difference I can make to all that misery and chaos.' The reply was a shock, but it should be the banner under which anyone trying to improve anything marches. 'Don't be so arrogant! You can only make a tiny fraction of difference. But if you do not make it, nobody else will.'

This book sets out our experience and our techniques for making that first small difference, and building bigger differences from it. Top-down change rarely produces sustainable change and wholly beneficial change. As Mikhail Gorbachev's memoir of his life argues vividly, it was not the triumph of the West that destroyed the Soviet Union; it was the people's one-by-one withdrawal of their consent to be governed by it. So it is with all genuine improvement. It is the product of each individual's determination to do better, joined in that determination by an ever-growing circle of others.

The question always lurks, however, why change is necessary. The answer is seldom as obvious as it is in Yemen or it was in Bangladesh and the Soviet Union. At the level of your own comfortable country or workplace, why make changes? Is change, itself, simply a Western obsession driven by ideas of the perfectibility of humanity and earthly life which might even be seen as blasphemous elsewhere in the world? In these difficult and dangerous times, it is a fair question.

The answer, whilst neither simple nor wholly secure, is that most people seek an even balance between their system of governance, their spirituality and their material wellbeing. The balance can be reasonably – but not completely – easy to strike. It is so in many Western-style democracies, where a Christian history often emphasizes sharp distinction between spiritual and secular political issues. Or as in, say, Saudi Arabia, it can be a matter of constant strain between absolute monarchy, a powerful and strictly orthodox form of Islam, Wahhabism, and the desire for material prosperity for a rapidly growing population. In Islam, there is no divide between religion and state. But, even in Saudi Arabia, the accommodation of all three forces demands change, however gradual. And the pressure behind that change is greatly increased by globalization.

GLOBALIZATION

There are many aspects of globalization: the globalization of communication, of culture, of finance, of technology and much else besides. In this book we are primarily dealing with the impact of economic globalization.

Historians now remind us that globalization is not new. Up to the First World War, we had the globalization of empires: the British, Austro-Hungarian, Ottoman, Romanov, French, German, Italian, Belgian. Whilst they could hardly be said to have promoted fair trade, they did offer the open borders, low or absent tariffs, secure currency values and safe havens for overseas investment of capital that made the year 1914 a peak for volumes of international trade that stood unsurpassed for most of the 20th century.

There are plenty of critics of globalization. Whether they are the marchers or rioters who provide the mood music for every meeting of the world's richest and most powerful nations, the G7, or whether they are authors of the many luridly titled books on the subject – try *The Silent Takeover* by Noreena Hertz or Viviane Forrester's *The Economic Horror* or *No Logo* by Naomi Klein – there is no shortage of voices decrying the inequity, cultural homogenization and empty materialism some associate with globalization.

However, other economically literate commentators, notably Philippe Legrain,[1] present a convincing case that globalization has the power to raise living standards for most people, quicker than anything else. Legrain points out that, in 1960, the national wealth of North Korea was double that of neighbouring South Korea. Their positions are not only now reversed, but the contrast in living standards could hardly be more extreme. North Korea opted out of the world free-trade system. (It is important to note that nations are still free to do so.) South Korea whole-heartedly opted in. The results are spectacular, visible not only in dry, economic data, but in all the softer indices of human welfare and happiness as well. The fact that the average South Korean is nine times richer than 35 years ago has fed through into an increase in life expectancy from 54 years for those born in 1960 to 75 years today. China, Taiwan, Singapore, Thailand, Indonesia, Malaysia and Japan are not far behind in economic growth. In the past few years, India has joined in and its bandwagon is rolling ever faster. What made its wheels turn was the abandonment of tariff barriers against international trade.

For anyone who cares about the wellbeing of their fellow human beings, these things are a cause for celebration. It is deeply regrettable that other countries, particularly in Africa, have not yet joined the list. Prosperity through increased trade has one almost magical property. More trade begets more wealth for everyone involved. We are not dividing up a finite cake, but creating the ingredients for bigger and bigger cakes. According to Legrain, open economies double in size every 16 years, while closed ones do so only every century, by which time the living standards of the open economies would have grown eight-fold. But global trade, globalization, increases the pressure for productivity. It increases the demand not just for improvement, but continuous improvement. Someone, somewhere, has always found a better way to do things; a better product. While new jobs and new wealth are always being created in open economies, the stress of adjustment as old ones go elsewhere, to places where they do things better or cheaper, is nonetheless acute.

THE BRITISH EXPERIENCE

The United Kingdom, we believe, is a uniquely valuable laboratory for testing all this and deducing from the experiment lessons that have some value for others. The British embarked first in the world on the adventure of the Industrial Revolution, some time in the latter part of the 18th century, more than 200 years ago. The British Empire, at least in its mature economic form, was built as much on that explosion of productive capacity as it was on the wanderlust of generations of islanders who had nowhere to go that was not overseas.

We were also among the first to set foot in the post-industrial world, the so-called knowledge economy, around 1980. The trauma of the Industrial Revolution is recorded in the writing of a host of Victorian authors, from Dickens' *Hard Times* to Elizabeth Gaskell's *North and South* to the philosophizing of Carlyle and John Ruskin. Until recently, the scars were still plain to see in rows of mean inner-city housing, industrial wastelands and belching chimneys. All that has gone, to the regret of very few.

But the scars of rapid mutation from a moribund industrial society into an economy based on free trade – a knowledge economy of mostly invisible products like financial services, insurance, 'intellectual capital', culture – are still easy to trace. Figure 1.1 shows the proportion of people in Britain in employment over the period 1971 to 2006.

Look at the years around 1980. The proportion of the working-age population who had jobs fell by more than six percentage points in about three years. That was the effect of a new government led by Margaret Thatcher, abandoning economic protectionism; abruptly ceasing to prop up failing industries with money raised from taxation; privatizing a host of activities which had, over time, attached themselves to the public sector; and emphasizing productivity much more than social security. After a blip or two in the early 1990s, a period of experiment with the new economy now derided as 'boom and bust', the proportion of working-age people who are employed in Britain has settled into a steadily rising path. It is, today, among the world's highest at around 75 per cent, with 70 per cent of women working and an overall target of 80 per cent set for the next few years.

There is no very obvious reason why the United Kingdom should still be so powerful an economy. The advantage of early industrialization had largely been lost by the latter part of the 19th century, when France, Germany and the United States of America had all mobilized their greater natural resources to overtake Britain. Britain is a small island, with few natural resources (not forgetting the cushioning of the transition to a knowledge economy by the discovery of oil in the North Sea) and a very large population for its size. Sixty million Britons today are tightly packed in an

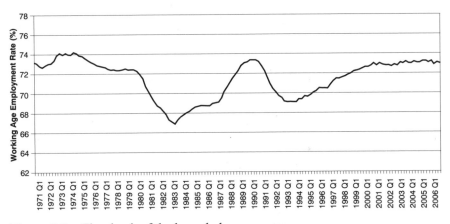

Figure 1.1   The shock of the knowledge economy
Source: Department for Work and Pensions, UK

area of about a quarter of a million square kilometres; a density of 240 people per km² compared with India at 310 people per km², France with only 109 per km² or the United States with just 28 people per km². It is by no means the most densely populated country on earth, but the comparison does show how some others may place greater reliance on natural resources for their prosperity. We walk a tightrope with no safety net. Manufacturing which, a quarter century ago, made up nearly 30 per cent of our economic output now accounts for only 15 per cent. But the value of its products has remained about the same. Financial services, in the wake of the 'Big Bang' which opened the City of London to less regulated, computer-dependent, 24 hours-a-day trading in money, commodities and shares, now account for a fifth of our annual earnings. £4.5 trillion a year of the world's money passes through London, contributing healthily to a £1 trillion a year economy as a little of every transaction remains on the City's sticky fingers.

It is not economics as we used to know it, but it is an economics which favours the fleet-of-foot, the highly educated and the skilled. Festoons of trend lines are produced every year in the United Kingdom, showing the steep decline in availability of jobs for those who have little to offer by way of skills and qualifications. Slashing across them are lines showing the growth of jobs in the professions, management, science, the arts: anything and everything that demands a university degree or at least an advanced technological diploma.

The unskilled jobs are increasingly being done for very little money by immigrants. Some of the growing number of skilled jobs are done by immigrants too. While unemployment is low and the retirement age is being pushed up and up to keep the experienced and skilled in work for longer, the number of people on disability benefits has increased from 1 million to 2.5 million in a couple of decades. It beggars belief that they are all disabled to an extent that bars them from work or that they would be seen as such in poorer parts of the world. It is much more likely that many of these people have been left behind by the knowledge economy, with too little education or skill even to form the foundation on which new and greater capability could be built.

Britain is not alone in this. We have seen much the same thing in Australia, Canada – all those places where the new global economy is otherwise hugely boosting earnings and standards of living.

The lesson to be drawn from the catastrophic loss of jobs illustrated in Figure 1.1 is that it pays to prepare very carefully for the transition to open markets and the knowledge economy. In Britain, we had no model we could follow. We were guided only by economic theory. It took both faith and the determination of the Iron Lady to persist with the new economic policy in the face of such dire early results. And it should be remembered that the collapse of the employment market rarely, if ever, takes place without other unpleasant effects. In Britain, we had a parallel collapse of the value of the currency; the failure of many companies; and acute labour unrest. In a less stable political environment, and one in which a less sophisticated population could not readily see that the old ways led only to decline, the probable result would have been political revolution.

In the best possible scenario, all the building blocks for success in a free-trade global market should be in place before the doors are opened. Legrain describes how this seldom happens. Most countries opt for protection of their industries behind tariff barriers, presuming that this will enable them to grow strong in preparation for more competitive international exposure. Legrain calls this policy 'mercantilism'. He points out that even apparently very successful economies do it to some extent. The United States of America, for example, carries on most of its open international trade with its immediate neighbours, Mexico and Canada, behind tariff barriers which embrace all three. All others get a less cosy deal. Much the same might be said of the European Union. 'Global' trade is often continental or regional in reality.

If you have sufficient wealth and potential for creating wealth close to hand, regional mercantilism may work, at least for a while. However, the evidence suggests that for really spectacular changes in economic health to be achieved, the risks of genuine free trade need to be faced.

The model shown in Figure 1.2 shows the factors which most critically affect productivity and the ability to compete globally. Fundamental to success in raising productivity are five main elements, listed across the base of the diagram. There is a tendency in our country, and in others where we have worked, to highlight skills above the rest.

THE ROLE OF SKILLS AND PRODUCTIVITY

In a recent British government report,[2] skills were identified as accounting for about one-fifth of our productivity deficit with the world's top producers, notably the United States and France. One-fifth is not a negligible amount and, indeed, this book concentrates mainly on showing how to remedy that gap. However, it is important that deficits in skills are not addressed alone. One reason why governments seem prone to doing so may be that skills are usually identified as the province of the less well educated and the less economically successful. 'They' lack the skills that 'we' need to assure prosperity.

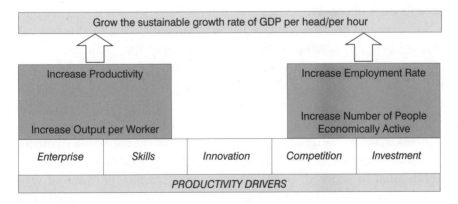

Figure 1.2   Productivity and growth are the result of five key drivers
Source: UK Treasury

We need to scotch this presumption right now. It is true that in most societies, intellectual endeavour and prowess are rated higher on the social scale than manual skill. Many countries have education systems which segregate the supposed thinkers from the toilers at ages between about 11 and 14, either within large comprehensive schools or in different schools. 'Other people's children' are destined to become car mechanics and construction workers, while ours will glide effortlessly into a clean, white shirt and a seat behind a desk in an air-conditioned office, there to earn a large salary with the minimum of sweat.

The British government among others has striven for years to create what it calls 'parity of esteem' between learning to refine intellectual capability and learning skills. It has made some progress, despite occasional recidivistic outbursts when the route through academic examinations to university is described by a politician as 'the golden road'.

This is not a harmless social affectation. Skills deficits are not an excuse for political and economic elites to blame those less fortunate or less powerful than themselves. Skill is a vital attribute for everyone involved in successful economic activity; the marriage of brain, eye and hand the hallmark of real capability in most walks of life. Whilst the 'Asian tigers' are not devoid of snobbery, it is not an accident that, for example, in Japan, skill is revered; the great craftsman celebrated as a Living National Treasure.

The real lesson of Figure 1.2 is that, to succeed in globalized markets, governments, employers, educators, labour unions, whole populations need to work in concert.

Success must be celebrated, rather than allowing what Australians call 'the tall poppy syndrome' to flourish, where those that push to excel are cut off at the knee as soon as their heads rise above the level of the crowd. We all have to save to create capital. We all need skills of appropriate kinds whether we lead a company or a country, or whether we are making and building things. Winners in the globalized world are co-operators. Winners in the globalized world respect and value the capability of others.

Productivity, itself, needs a little unpicking. Figure 1.2 suggests, rightly, that to succeed, countries must coax high proportions of their populations into work and provide the means for them to contribute a great deal of economic value when they are at work. This is undoubtedly true. The creation of high economic value demands success in a whole range of matters which are, in effect, the operational expressions of the characteristics listed across the base of Figure 1.2. These include the availability of excellent equipment, good management, environments refreshing and healthy enough for people to sustain high performance, freedom to criticize and propose improvement, good health and nutrition among working people, the availability of childcare to release women into the workforce.... The list is endless and it includes political and social factors as well as those which are directly economic.

It is with that in mind that we need to look at Figure 1.3, which shows the relative productivity of some different countries, for each hour worked.

We often look at this chart with some surprise. Our holiday experiences of the sleepy villages of rural France, for example, where pretty much all activity except the preparation and consumption of a wonderful lunch often seems to stop during the peak hours of the day, are at odds with the notion of high productivity. Yet it appears that when they are at work, the French are highly efficient and effective at producing economic value.

We might also question how it is that social democracies like those of Scandinavia rub shoulders at the top table with economies which are redder in tooth and claw – more 'devil take the hindmost' – like the United States. Looking beyond our chart, how is it that Italy is a relatively high performer, when it does very badly in what most people identify as a key attribute of economic strength in a globalized world, the ability to produce a high proportion of university graduates in each

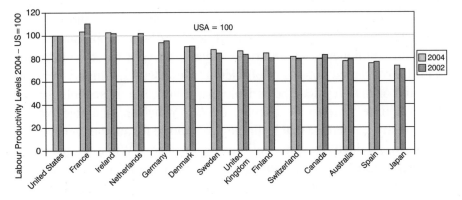

Figure 1.3   Productivity gap
Source: OECD

generation of young people? And why does the grandfather of all tiger economies, Japan, apparently perform badly? The answer is, of course, that beyond the simple equation of 'More people in work + Efficiency at work = High productivity' many other elements are in play. The global-ized world is a more complex world than the old nostrums about economic success – 'buy cheap and sell dear' and the rest – can describe.

It is a fair bet that the concern for human rights, healthcare, decent housing, equality of opportunity, care of the elderly, education and every other aspect of democratic fairness, which is to be found to an extraordi-nary degree in Scandinavia, contributes to high economic productivity. Contrary to the stereotypes, the Scandinavians score very highly in recent international surveys of happiness and wellbeing. They work effectively because they know they are getting a fair deal and their contribution to national wealth is appreciated. High levels of tax and a large public sector apparently do nothing to dispel this conviction.

Similarly, we can speculate fairly safely that high productivity in the United States is related to the presence of a large, highly motivated first- or second-generation immigrant population which a low-tax environ-ment helps to provide with tangible benefits from their labour, and a host of rags-to-riches examples helps convince that enterprise can transform their prospects and those of their children.

Japan is not all Toyota, Mitsubishi and Canon. It is a land of small farmers and small, primitive factories. It is a land where many people are occupied in seemingly unproductive jobs like bowing to customers as they enter shops. In Italy, it is possible for the dignitaries of a traditionally Communist city like Bologna to boast convincingly that they have 'a tech-nological culture', in which dozens of scattered workshops make high-precision components which are eventually brought together to make, against all accepted notions of efficient manufacturing, a highly success-ful brand of motorcycle. And in Bologna, technical high schools, spend-ing seven times as much per pupil as the *licei* which are 'the golden road' to university, perpetuate that technological culture for another generation.

In short, productivity is not entirely what it seems. While it must be the case that some of the astonishingly keenly priced goods we now buy from emerging economies have been produced in exploitative sweatshops, the pressures on companies and countries to do better for their working people are plain to see beneath the surface of the productivity charts.

NATIONAL SKILLS STRATEGIES

If long-term efficiency is not a powerful enough incentive, other facets of globalization, such as the risk of real-time media exposure, rising environmental awareness and shareholder power, pile on the pressure to run ethical businesses and ethical nation states. If the experience of South Korea is any guide, the media glare of the Olympic Games in Beijing will have a significant impact on social freedoms and political rights in China. And, while the relationship is not as direct as once was imagined, democratization and economic success are interconnected.

The imperatives of open competition, trade and productivity are very strong. They are strong enough to ensure that most of the countries we know either have a 'national skills strategy' or want one. Usually it contains many or most of these things:

- nursery education to ease working mothers' childcare responsibilities and allow them to work;
- concentration on literacy and numeracy in primary-level education;
- skills programmes in secondary-level education, alongside academic subjects;
- investment in technical and vocational education and training (TVET) to boost the quality and availability of skills among young people over the age of about 16;
- emphasis on improving work-based learning, including career-preparation programmes like apprenticeship;
- diversification of university courses to include 'non-traditional' vocational disciplines;
- welfare-to-work and upskilling programmes for people of working age;
- remedial literacy, numeracy and skills programmes for older workers whose schooling may have been inadequate for modern conditions;
- programmes to bring people who were once seen as excluded from work into the workforce, including disabled people, prisoners, people recovering from mental illness and young people who have dropped out of school;
- language and qualification-conversion programmes for immigrants.

In our country and in a number of others we know, enormous state investment has been accompanied by the introduction of tight measures of performance. Skills strategies are often peppered with targets, key performance indicators, standards and talk of outcomes rather than outputs, which once would have been the sole province of company reports rather than government plans. Skills strategies, in other words, have a tendency to become narrowly instrumental, in a way that our earlier discussion of productivity in a globalized world might suggest is unhelpful. Culture, in our experience, is as important to achievement as is performance.

TECHNICAL AND VOCATIONAL EDUCATION AND TRAINING (TVET)

We believe there is an optimum form for a TVET system effectively delivering skills. It does not exist everywhere. In countries where elements are missing, our experience is that their want is felt and that, within the real or perceived confines of local culture and habit, steps are taken to fill that want. It is possible to provide key elements in different ways. The model we show in Figure 1.4 is derived from the United Kingdom pattern, but even here, there are important differences in delivery between, for example, England and Scotland.

At the heart of the model are providers offering education and training. To one side is a system for delivering qualifications employers want, which are reliable and internationally portable by their holders. On the other is a system for guaranteeing good service to learners and other stakeholders and for stimulating the continuous improvement demanded for success in the globalized economy. Many countries are weak or wholly deficient in at least one of the three elements of the model. Our own country often shows a fatal tendency to misrepresent what is relatively simple for the would-be-learner, at the point of individual access, as a spider's web of corporate bodies and lines of relationship. This is not helpful.

Let us unpack each of the rings; first, the providers. As in many other countries, it was assumed in Britain until quite recently that all significant

Figure 1.4   A model for TVET
Source: © Sherlock and Perry, 2007

TVET providers would be publicly owned. That presumption was shed by government some years ago. The reason was that, while many young people or adults see no barriers in the way of attending a college, there are many who now must be included in a skills strategy but who will not do so. They include people for whom schooling was a torment of continuous failure so that they lack the basics for further learning, and people whose employers cannot spare them during working hours and who are too tired or disinclined to study in the evenings. In Britain, those categories, and others including disability, confinement for offending behaviour or the limitations imposed by specialist occupations like the armed services, add up to an awful lot of people.

The British government's response was to redefine public services. Rather than services provided solely by the public sector and usually funded through taxation, public services in Britain can now be provided on contract by private, charitable or public sector organizations. The choice depends on which is the cheapest, the most efficient and the most adaptable to the rapidly changing needs of a modern globalized economy and society. The result of this diversification is that TVET providers, including public sector colleges, are now much more varied in character and size. They are much more geared to a customer-service approach to learners, offering services wherever and whenever they are in demand. Of the 1,500 or so TVET providers remaining in England alone, around 250 are large colleges and the rest are employers training their own staff; specialist training companies ranging from the very large to the tiny;

charities serving particular areas of need, including disability, a history of criminal behaviour or of under-privilege; professional bodies; chambers of commerce and other trade associations; local and central government; and trades unions.

In these circumstances there are very few learning needs that cannot be met. But consider the impact on accountability for public funding. A large, private work-based training provider will place learners in several thousand small employers. They will be scattered in ones and twos over a wide area, perhaps across the whole country. They have to be visited regularly to ensure that they are learning alongside work, and that their progress towards a qualification is monitored and assessed. The problems of control are as challenging as the advantages of this proliferation and easy availability of learning opportunities are compelling. This rainbow coalition of providers of public services is as vitally necessary, as complex and as difficult to control as the open global economy itself.

It follows that the means of shaping this provision, so that it does, indeed, offer a service in the public interest, need to be equally sophisticated, diverse and flexible. They, too, will need to change as circumstances change. A frequently recurring debate in Britain has been around the level of trust which appropriately can be placed in providers. There have been examples of large-scale fraud, both in public sector and private sector providers. The trigger has invariably been a government initiative which either imposes so unfair a demand for growth or cost reduction that some providers feel it imperative to break or bend the rules, or a scheme so open to exploitation that criminal conspiracies spring up expressly for the purpose.

The lesson is that to engage almost everybody in a society in contributing to a booming economy, new learning needs always have to be satisfied and that this cannot be done without experiment and risk. The secret of success is to ensure that the controls over providers are proportionate and that the level of risk injected by government in making progress stops short of being foolhardy. To quote former President Reagan of the United States, 'Trust, but verify.'

In Britain, verification of different kinds is provided in the two outer rings of our model. They are, in effect, the twin guarantors of the public interest. The ring containing the qualifications structure is most often found in some form in other countries.

English TVET qualifications conform to standards set by employers. Those employers gather together in 25 Sector Skills Councils, responsible for developing occupational standards. We have seen similar structures in Canada; in Australia, where their number has recently been reduced sharply to cut the number of boundary disputes; and in Saudi Arabia where standards were developed by a government agency in partnership with a British company with a long-term stake in the country and two British awarding bodies. These standards are necessary but not sufficient to guarantee good TVET; a misconception we have found to be common in many parts of the world.

Occupational standards are not entirely straightforward to design, however well chosen the employer representatives on sector councils may be. The employers willing and able to release senior staff for an altruistic enterprise tend to be large and, therefore, usually not typical of a work sector. The employers in, say, petrochemicals, will be big and few. In construction, most work is carried out by small contractors or sole traders whose interests and concerns are unlikely to be the same as those of an international civil engineering company which may quickly spring to government's mind when representatives of the industry are being sought. Rapidly changing technologies also cause problems. It is hard to keep occupational standards up to date. There are dangers, too, in specifying tasks and skills too narrowly. What may seem commonsense in one workplace can appear as a clumsy straitjacket in another.

Building the standards into TVET qualifications are awarding bodies. In Britain there are nearly 150 of these, offering many thousands of different awards. British awarding bodies are often international, providing qualifications which can become generally accepted global benchmarks. The City and Guilds of London Institute has its roots deep in the tradition of ancient craft guilds, but its international qualifications are so well established that, in some parts of the world, a vocational qualification has the generic name of 'A cityandguilds'. Some of these awarding bodies are not-for-profit, charitable organizations. Others are commercial companies.

Regulating English awards is a government body, the Qualifications and Curriculum Authority (QCA). It ensures that awarding bodies reliably assure the rigour of the qualifications they confer, and that these qualifications match the occupational standards. QCA also operates a national credit accumulation and transfer system that breaks up curricula into convenient packages, particularly for adult part-time study. It ensures that units of study easily can be built on without loss of time, when a learner moves to a new place or a new job.

Even within the United Kingdom, these arrangements are not uniform. In Scotland, the Scottish Qualifications Authority (SQA) is awarding body, regulator and controller of credit accumulation and transfer. It takes care to minimize the obvious potential for conflicts of interest. The resulting 'one-stop shop', with one organization occupying the whole of one ring of our model, has made SQA a popular partner for other countries which need access to a secure system of technical and vocational awards. Among them is China.

In other countries, the government itself issues TVET awards. In yet others, like Australia, agencies of state governments license providers themselves to make awards.

Beneath all these variations, the essential functions which must be efficiently fulfilled are much the same. Differences and difficulties arise when the matter of portability, vital to learners, is dealt with. Australian TVET awards, for example, vary in prestige according to the reputation of the body that issues them. They are not necessarily accepted by employers in another state of Australia, let alone in another country. Balanced against those potential or actual problems are simplicity and probably a lack of bureaucracy in comparison with those British systems which are widely used internationally and which carry both the guarantees of an independent, specialist awarding body and a government agency behind it. Choices have to be made in relation to cost, ease of use and international comparability and credibility.

The third ring of the model, quality assessment and improvement, lies at the heart of this book. There is no doubt that providers themselves must, in the end, take full responsibility for the quality of the service they offer to learners. Nobody else can be there, supervising what is going on, all the time. Nobody else can make the changes necessary to drive forward continuous improvement. What can be done, however, is to offer independent external monitoring and advice which is informed by an international and national perspective on what is needed for success in the global skills market, rather than the solely local one which most providers will have. What can also be done is to introduce 'carrots and sticks': motivations to do better, such as awards and celebrations, and sanctions for those who cannot or will not improve, such as restriction or withdrawal of public funding.

Such things can be, but need not be, highly controversial. In a number of countries where we have worked, criticism which may be seen as confrontational is contrary to religious or cultural expectations. It is bad manners to say that someone else's performance is lacking. Elsewhere, society is understood to be built on a pyramid of families, clans and tribes, where obligations to kin override all other considerations. Open and honest criticism, however constructive and well intentioned, is impossible in those circumstances, eliminating along with it any notion of an independent view.

These inhibitions are doubled in force if, as in England, it is suggested that real impetus for improvement can be found in publishing the findings of an independent quality assessment on the internet, literally for all the world to see. However beneficial open publication might be in spreading good practice and informing potential learners so that they flock to the best providers and further reinforce their success, in many countries initial resistance to the idea is very powerful. 'Identify and celebrate' might be well received. However, in very many cases the only honest outcome would be 'name and shame', which emphatically would not.

We have described in this chapter some of the hurdles that TVET must jump if it is to provide the skills an open economy needs. It must be easily accessible to all. It must engage people who do not want to learn, have very little experience of learning and for whom the experiences they once had were thoroughly disagreeable. It must reach out to these reluctant learners where they live and work, rather than just opening the doors to a well-equipped, well-adapted college. It must offer learning in convenient packages, which can be fitted in alongside daily life and work and which closely relate theory and practice. It must be endlessly flexible to accommodate individual circumstances and preferences, as well as technological change and business practice, and yet it must retain coherence of form and rigour so that it qualifies for a widely respected award. It must respond promptly to the new demands imposed by the employers and governments that pay for TVET, changing ever more quickly as they ride the stormy surges of the global economy.

Contradictions, frustrations and unreasonable demands abound. In our experience, few providers cope with them well entirely on their own. Performance, in most of the countries we have visited, is regarded as disappointing. Learners drop out of work-based learning programmes as often because they have moved to a better job as they do because their learning programme was inadequate or unsuitable. And yet a failure to complete an expensive learning programme successfully is a failure to add to the national stock of skills, however plausible the reason.

The problems can be overcome.

Case Study 1

Unipart plc: an exemplary learning organization

Twenty years ago, Unipart was a subsidiary of a state-owned motor vehicle manufacturer. For this single customer, its parent company, Unipart made and distributed spare parts. Located outside Oxford, Unipart presented a stark contrast with the ancient university which gives the city its fame. Far from being a centre of excellence, Unipart's parent, British Leyland, had a reputation for poor-quality products, low productivity and bad labour relations. In 1987 it operated what was described as 'Britain's worst factory', its notoriously unproductive night shift earning the tag of the best place to sleep in Oxford.

The British government then sold off Unipart to a new company owned by its former managers. They were inspired by the work of Deming and others on 'lean manufacturing' and the warning of management writer Peter Drucker: 'To survive... an organization will have to renew its learning every three years.' These positive incentives were reinforced by the emerging relationship with Unipart of two of the world's most important potential customers, Toyota and Honda. Taking a lead from these successful global companies, Unipart set about re-creating itself as 'a learning organization'. This is defined as one in which every employee, from the most senior to the most junior, accepts a responsibility to acquire new knowledge and skills continuously, contributing to ever-rising quality and efficiency for the benefit of the company as a whole.

There was resistance among some of the Unipart workforce, which was often led by unions. Derecognition helped to remove some of the major barriers. While the vision was clear, Unipart found it hard to find the advice it wanted to help people at every level of the business. Commercial training providers were found to be insufficiently specific in addressing the particular issues arising daily on the shop floor. Universities were seen as training for the national stock of skilled people, rather than meeting Unipart's needs. Many consultants were found to be strong on theory but weak on practical implementation. Unipart had to find its own way out of its difficulties. It did so by listening carefully to its staff.

In 1993, the company launched a 'corporate university' called Unipart U. It aimed at making learning fast, relevant to the real problems of work and, by encouraging personal discovery and sharing experience among employees, motivational. Many Unipart employees had low levels of educational qualification and were doing manual jobs in warehousing and logistics. Learning in Unipart U had to transform the attitudes of the most sceptical or fearful, as well as offering new capabilities. When people could see that learning would immediately help them in their work, and that their wider experience of life was as highly valued as any formal education, they became enthusiastic supporters of Unipart U.

Unipart U is based on a clear philosophy called 'The Unipart Way'. It has several key components, including 'The University on the shop floor' – drop-in classrooms in the warehouse; 'Our Contribution Counts' (OCC) circles, where employees learn problem-solving techniques and develop new ways of improving company performance; a best-practice database online; e-learning and work-based assessment facilities; and extension of the same principles to Unipart suppliers as a form of supply chain quality management.

Today, Unipart provides logistic services to many successful global companies including Airbus, Vodafone, Hewlett Packard, Jaguar and retailers Halfords and Homebase. It distributes 750,000 products through 7,000 outlets in 100 countries. It claims to offer the best product availability in the industry with zero defects. It is both profitable and productive. Its chief executive describes its learning programme, Unipart U, as 'the platform from which we will see the future of our company'.

Notes

1   Legrain, P (2002) *Open World: The truth about globalization*, Abacus, London
2   Leitch, A (2006) *Prosperity for All in the Global Economy – World Class Skills*, TSO, London

2

Standards and frameworks

Starting off a long-term process of continuous improvement in TVET demands clear and reliable identification of how good we are today. This is not always easy. Most of us believe we are doing a good job, or at least doing our best. Few of us really know what excellent performance, in the global context, looks like. How pretentious it is even to consider such a notion! Few of us are really fired up by the idea of becoming the very best. We cannot see such high ambition as realistic for us. There are a host of incentives to carry on just as we are.

Challenged by an argument that the performance we are achieving today will not be good enough to win against the constantly rising competition at work in the open global market, a first response is often 'OK. Show me the standard I have to meet.' A central conclusion we have reached through experience is that this is the wrong place to start.

Standards certainly have their place. In the previous chapter we touched on the system of occupational standards that exists in a growing number of countries. Where doing a job in one, specific, way is critical to people's safety or to the long-term durability of a product, an occupational standard is not only desirable but essential. We do not want a technician to find new ways to service an aircraft engine. We want the job done exactly as Rolls-Royce or General Electric intended. We do not want a bricklayer to experiment with the mix of cement used to hold our houses together. We do not want staff at our banks to use creative accounting methods when they safeguard and manage our money. We want unimaginative compliance with the regulations laid down by a national financial authority.

Standards are, in essence, tight performance specifications laid down by someone else. They may be the result of experience or calculation but they are meant to be obeyed; not neglected or exceeded. If you fill your car with oil above the 'maximum' mark on the dipstick on the grounds that lubrication is good and so the more you have the better, you will destroy the engine. The standard is defined as the range of levels between the 'minimum' and 'maximum' marks.

Somewhat confusingly, there are quality frameworks which are misnamed as standards. The European Framework for Quality Management (EFQM) is exactly what it says it is: a framework. It defines broad areas of activity which are common to most organizations and against which you are invited to assess your performance. You may decide that you are excellent or satisfactory or not yet good enough in each one. Yet EFQM lies beneath several business excellence models. The British Midlands Excellence 'standard' is not, in fact, a standard. The British Investors in People 'standard' is not a standard. Both are measures of the threshold below which no self-respecting organization should fall. Neither, however, seeks to put a cap on innovation or achievement above that threshold. Indeed, they encourage them. That is the kind of framework or guideline which, we believe, is the only one fitted to powering continuous improvement.

Think of it this way. A ship is moving with the tide. Even if the ship stops its engines, the tide keeps on flowing and the ship goes along with it. The tide represents the ever-shifting level of performance in developing skills required just to survive in the global economy. What is satisfactory today will be inadequate tomorrow. Our ship has to go faster than the tide because if we merely drift with it the rudder does not bite and we have no control. Collision with the rest of the drifting crowd is almost inevitable, followed, at best, by falling behind. What we need is a combination of stimulus, guidance and help to go as far and as fast as we can. The engines have to run powerfully and continuously if we are to beat the running tide; to excel.

We call our solution to the challenge of securing continuous improvement in learning The Transformational Diamond (Figure 2.1). The four keywords, four As – Aspiration, Assessment, Assistance, Accumulation – are easy to remember and should be present in any useful continuous quality improvement scheme for TVET. They echo the four Cs that classify the quality of the diamond on your finger: carat, clarity, colour and cut.

Figure 2.1   The Transformational Diamond
Source: © Sherlock and Perry, 2007

As we show near the end of the book, it is possible to begin your own quest for excellence at any point of The Transformational Diamond. The model is infinitely flexible and culturally adaptable. It has to be if it is to be useful in carving out distinctive positions for each organization or region or country competing in the open global market. There is always a multitude of different ways to achieve the same end. In this chapter, we begin where Britain began; with Assessment. We do not presume that this is the best place to begin in some other cultures, but the moment will always come when it is needed.

SHAPING A JUDGEMENT

To raise a point in order only to discard it, it is possible to carry out quality assessment without reference to a dedicated framework. Traditional British inspection, as we described it in our Introduction, was often based on the judgement of expert practitioners alone, without reference to any written framework. In some areas it still is. The inspection of every aspect of the life of prison inmates in this country was guided by a halfway-house between no framework at all and one that used detailed definitions. It was described as a set of 'expectations'.

We have written and used several TVET assessment frameworks before the one shown later in this chapter and we recommend strongly that a framework should always be used. These are our reasons:

- Developing a written framework allows widespread consultation to help confirm that it is appropriate.
- A written framework helps everyone believe that quality assessment is transparent and honest.
- A written framework can be used both for self-assessment by organizations themselves as well as independent confirmation that the conclusions are accurate.
- A written framework defines the terms for a professional dialogue between TVET practitioners and quality assessors, making a meeting of minds easier to achieve.
- A written framework allows disputed conclusions from quality assessment to be questioned and resolved.
- A written framework can act as a definition of good practice.

We believe it is a basic right that everyone should clearly understand and be given the opportunity to contribute to the basis on which judgements are made about the quality of their work. Unless a person or an organization is genuinely convinced that those judgements are correct and robust enough to withstand natural doubts, they will not be accepted. Unless they are accepted, nothing will be done to build on strengths or, still more, to remedy weaknesses. And unless quality assessment leads to action, it is a waste of time and resources.

We need also to scotch one other possible misapprehension in relation to the use of quality assessment frameworks. They are not checklists. Ticking a yes/no box will not suffice to determine quality. The reason is perhaps obvious. If, for example, a framework includes the need for evaluation of a quality improvement strategy, in order to tell how effective it is in making things better for learners, we have to know more than whether a policy document exists or not. We have to make a judgement about how appropriate and clearly defined that policy is and whether it has had a real impact on operations. Making that judgement will demand evidence whose importance can be checked and weighed. That is a whole lot more complex and potentially valuable than ticking the yes/no box. Without disparaging auditors, we should emphasize here that there is a real distinction to be made between inspection, or quality assessment, and audit. Any decision involving many complex factors will rely on judgement. We are making difficult judgements about how good and how useful is TVET. We are not auditing compliance with a set of rules or checking the existence of processes and procedures.

How do we define 'quality'? What is 'improvement'? There is a thread always to be found in human affairs that measures benefit mainly from a personal point of view: what is good for me is good for everybody.

Getting away from an egocentric view of quality is challenging. It is the motive force beyond the invention of 'standards', with their aura of objectivity. But, as we have argued, standards impose limitations which are unendurable among those who aspire to excellence. Is excellence therefore to be defined as the preference of an elite, as it might be in *haute couture*? Is excellence to be defined as the judgement of the majority, as it might be in setting the value of a currency or a company's shares?

In learning, neither will suffice. It is manifestly absurd to argue (as might once have been argued) that the only or predominant model of 'a good school' should be Eton or other elite English fee-paying schools. Other schools, planned on different lines, do a better job for their particular clientele than Eton ever could or would wish to. It is equally absurd to argue that an ideal might be defined as an average as far as learning is concerned. Politicians everywhere wrestle with the conundrum of providing educational opportunities which are both inclusive of all comers and suited to fostering outstanding talents. Everyone accepts that both these requirements must be met, but how to ensure that the availability of learning opportunities and the operational decisions of institutions do not force them apart, make them mutually exclusive?

WHAT IS GOOD LEARNING?

Defining quality in learning – because learning is a basic human capability – is a political, cultural and technical minefield. Our experience is that an unsung hero in the British civil service got it triumphantly right in 1997. His or her definition was that quality in learning provision was to be judged by the level of benefit experienced by each individual learner. This definition works on a pragmatic level, a logical level, an ethical level and a technical level. After some initial parlaying, it works in just about every learning context.

Let us consider the benefits of using this definition:

- No teacher is likely to reject it.
- It rings the 'customer first' bell, now increasingly predominant in public services as well as private enterprise.
- 'Benefit' can usually be measured with some accuracy in the distance travelled between an initial assessment of knowledge or capability and another conducted after learning.
- A focus on the individual fits well with the differences in prior learning, prior experience and personal aspiration universally found among adult learners.
- It is susceptible to productive debate and agreement between teacher, learner, manager and independent assessor.

The shortcomings we have found in this definition are these:

- There are often multiple stakeholders in adult learning, not least employers and the state which often foot much of the bill.
- In some learning situations, improving the capability of a team of people is paramount, rather than that of an individual.
- It can be seen merely as a means of resolving conflict rather than securing agreement.

These difficulties have some weight. However, it is usually possible to argue convincingly that for the sponsor of learning to benefit, the learner must benefit first. It is usually possible to argue convincingly that effective teams are made up of effective individuals and that learning and team formation are distinct, if not entirely separate. Avoidance, rather than resolution, of conflict is to be preferred and the means of avoidance in authoritative quality assessment is to be found in the assembly of compelling evidence.

A decade of successful application of the definition of quality in learning as the level of benefit to the individual learner has convinced us that it is simple, elegant and workable. We have applied it across the full range of learning environments in England, as well as in several other countries. It has been adopted by yet other nations which have found it resolves a basic issue in a way that unites funding agencies, teachers and learners themselves. It is unreasonable to hope for more.

This quality criterion is now at the root of *The Common Inspection Framework* in England. Having worked on its evolution at every stage so far, we offer below a new version, which distils the elements we suggest are best fitted to adult learning and TVET.

A NEW FRAMEWORK

The Quality Assessment Framework for self-assessment and independent quality assessment

This framework asks six questions covering all aspects of learning. One of them prompts you to make a judgement about the overall quality of the learning experience of each learner. Under every question are indicators or types of evidence which might help you to answer. For some questions there are also 'where appropriate' statements which will apply in some, but not all, learning contexts. These indicators are not a checklist which must be completed. Many users of the framework will find other, equally valid, indicators of their own. The questions are arranged in four sections to cover all aspects of the learner's journey.

Overall effectiveness

1 How effective and efficient is the provision in meeting learners' needs; and why?

Achievement

2 Do learners achieve their learning goals?

Indicators to inform the answer to this question

- Learners' success in achieving challenging targets including qualifications, units of qualifications or progress towards employment or promotion.
- The quality of learners' written, oral and practical work, related to their learning goals.
- Learners' progress compared with their prior attainment and experience.
- The extent of learners' personal and learning skills.
- The trends over time in learners' achievement and retention rates in this provider.

And, where appropriate

- Learners' attainment of workplace skills.
- Learners' attendance and punctuality records.
- The consistency of high achievement and retention levels across all the areas of training.

The quality of learning provision

3 How effective are teaching, training and learning?

Indicators to inform the answer to this question

- The appropriateness of teaching, training and resources to help learners progress on their courses or programmes.
- The suitability, frequency and rigour of assessment.
- The speed and accuracy with which any additional learning needs are identified and met.
- The technical competence and up-to-date knowledge of teachers and trainers, at levels appropriate to the courses or programmes on which they teach.

- The extent to which lesson and course plans used by teachers and trainers provide learners with clear objectives and help them to learn methodically.
- The use of an appropriate variety of teaching methods to challenge, inspire and involve every learner.
- The effective use of assignments and practical work to help learners to understand how to apply the knowledge they have gained.
- The use of personalized learning by teachers and trainers to meet each individual learner's needs.
- The extent to which teachers and trainers ensure equality of opportunity and make positive use of the diversity of learners' backgrounds to enrich learning.

4 How well do programmes and courses meet the requirements and interests of learners?

Indicators to inform the answer to this question
- The extent to which courses and programmes match learners' aspirations and potential, building on their prior attainment and experience.
- The adaptability of courses and programmes to changing circumstances, technological developments and the requirements of employers.
- The range of courses and programmes readily available to learners.
- The coherence of courses and programmes and their ability to enable learners to progress as far and as fast as they are able.

And, where appropriate
- The extent to which multi-site provision and resources are effectively integrated to provide a coherent programme, including learning at work.

5 How well are learners guided and supported?

Indicators to inform the answer to this question
- The extent to which personal support, advice and guidance help each learner to progress and remain on the course or programme until it is complete.

- The quality, accessibility and impartiality of the information, advice and guidance which is offered to help learners to choose the programme, course or career that is right for them.
- The degree to which induction activities help learners to settle into study quickly, to understand their rights and duties and the particular demands of the course or programme.
- The accessibility of specialist support services for those who need them.
- The sensitivity of the personal guidance and support services which are provided, to the cultural backgrounds of every learner.

Leadership and management

6 **How effective are leadership and management in achieving outstanding outcomes for all?**

Indicators to inform the answer to this question

- The extent to which performance is monitored accurately and is continuously improved through appropriate quality assurance and assessment methods, including self-assessment which is informed by the views of all interested parties.
- The level of concern shown by leaders and managers at all levels to achieve continuous improvement and to provide learners with the best possible care, education and training.
- The effectiveness with which equality of opportunity and the value of diversity are promoted, and unfair discrimination is tackled, so that all learners achieve their full potential.
- The adequacy and appropriateness of staffing, achieved through good practice in recruitment, selection and continuous professional development.
- The regularity and rigour with which staff performance is monitored and improved to ensure that the service offered to learners is of the best possible quality.
- The accessibility and suitability of specialist equipment, learning resources and accommodation.
- The efficiency of use of all resources to aid learning.

- The clarity of direction given to everyone in the organization through well-defined strategic objectives and values that are fully understood, including by any subcontractors.
- The use of demanding targets for learner retention, achievement, progression and employment which are regularly met.
- The accuracy of data and management information and their routine use to improve the service to learners.
- The easy availability of clear, fair and swift processes to deal with appeals and complaints.
- The use of good practice examples from inside the organization and elsewhere, to raise the quality of the learning experience.

And, where appropriate
- The extent to which governors, trustees or other supervisory boards effectively oversee strategic direction and regularly monitor the quality of provision and their own performance.

© Sherlock and Perry, 2007

WHAT IS EVIDENCE?

The Quality Assessment Framework has the merit that it is short and simple enough to be put in the hands of every member of staff in a training organization. If not something for daily reference, it should be helpful to anyone needing to check every few weeks whether they are concentrating on the right things, setting the right priorities. It is not a thick, gloomy book of instructions useful only when some formal assessment procedure is in prospect. First and foremost, it is a prompt for everyone to help them develop excellent practice.

Its brevity, however, is likely to suggest more questions. You might well need to dig beneath its surface and to discuss and agree with your colleagues what it might mean for them. We have been involved in many such sessions; let us consider how some of the debates might run.

First is the vital matter of evidence. Effective use of the Quality Assessment Framework depends on being able to reach judgements which are reliable enough to form the basis for actions – some of which might be deeply unpopular with those they affect – and which are robust enough to withstand intelligent questioning. The framework is an instrument for building sincere agreement among people who respect one another. It is not an instrument for the imposition of arbitrary opinion and authority.

Some of this evidence will be objective and statistical. Any well-run learning organization should be able to provide secure data on, for example, the number of learners who began a course at a particular time; whether they completed it; whether they achieved the award they worked for; and what happened to them when they left, either before or after qualifying. Anyone assessing performance independently will be deeply sceptical about the organization that does not keep a firm grip on these basic facts about its customers. We will discuss the interpretation and management of data later in the book but, for the moment, we can assume that there will be some reliable numbers to give the beginnings of insight into organizational performance.

However, basing a judgement solely on achievement data would give a very impoverished view of effectiveness. Consider the results of a group of young learners attending a specialist academic institution. Let us say they had been carefully selected on the basis of their earlier academic results from among a very large field of candidates. Their examination performance would probably look very good. Almost all would have passed, most of them with flying colours. But what would that tell us about the value added by the institution? If the learners were high-fliers in the first place, intelligent and used to learning on their own, their years in a college or university might have contributed little more than fast internet access and some additional maturity and experience of life.

If, on the other hand, we found ourselves confronted by a list of very mediocre examination results, achieved by adults from very diverse and often deeply disadvantaged backgrounds, what then? It might be right to say that the institution had contributed a great deal to their progress and to their prospects in life, but we would nevertheless have to inquire further to find out just how much.

Statistical data guide the formulation of questions; they do not answer them with the level of certainty we need if the future of people and whole organizations is to depend on the responses.

Understanding that even apparently incontrovertible facts need unpicking if they are to be helpful in applying the Quality Assessment Framework opens up two new avenues. First, evidence which is useful for our purposes has to be drawn from several sources if it is to be considered reliable. It has to be 'triangulated' in inspection jargon, or based ideally on at least three independent pieces of information. Second, evidence might consist of a whole range of objective and subjective contributions. It may come in the form of statistics, interviews with learners, teachers or managers, records of meetings, policy documents and, centrally for our purposes, direct observation of the learning process as it happens.

For example, a quality assessor who is told by a group of learners that teachers are apathetic and often late or absent from lessons will undoubtedly be concerned. That concern will rise if the same picture emerges from a series of one-to-one interviews with learners. It will be heightened further if staff records show unusually high levels of absenteeism. Discussions with managers, with both the feedback from learners and the records on the table, may not only confirm that there are staffing problems which are having a serious impact on learning, but will often reveal the nature of those problems. Is the organization under new management, trying hard to recover from earlier underperformance, and is there evidence that things are now getting better? Is there unrest among staff, perhaps including a deep-seated labour dispute? Are senior managers, themselves, often absent, involved in work which, however worthwhile, has led them to neglect their duty to control the performance of their staff?

Under each of the 'Indicators to inform the answer to this question' which are used in a particular case, there needs to be a careful process of gathering facts, cross-checking and assembly into evidence. That evidence will first support a preliminary view about what may be happening and, following discussion and debate, a conclusion firm enough to act upon. And as the differing scenarios sketched out in the previous paragraph might suggest, that conclusion will itself be shaped by circumstance. 'Learners are', as our evidence has demonstrated, 'neglected by many teachers and becoming increasingly disaffected.' That is, in itself, a very significant problem and needs to be acknowledged as such. However, the way that problem is expressed and the weight given to it in reaching a judgement about the overall effectiveness of the learning provision will be influenced in some degree by whether managers recognize it and are working effectively to fix it, or whether it is the inevitable outcome of their own neglect.

AND WHY?

It follows that the first, overarching question in the Quality Assessment Framework will be the last to be answered. It is the sum of secure answers, backed by evidence, to all the other five questions. Just how good that evidence must be, and how good the answers, will become clear when we tackle the final phrase in the overarching question: 'and why?'

It is the most difficult part of the whole exercise and the most necessary. Being able to say why a learning organization is fulfilling or failing each learner's needs makes severe demands on the intelligence, experience and knowledge of those who do it. Without it, however, it is practically impossible to draw up a blueprint for continuous improvement.

Confronting the question 'why?' often takes courage. The answer may be that people in senior positions are not up to the job or not doing the job they are paid for. Even if they initiated a quality assessment in the first place, it is unlikely that criticism of their competence is the answer they were looking for. That is reason enough why many organizations are incapable of reaching an incisive view about their own performance and setting themselves on course for a better future, entirely on their own. Messages that need to have a hard edge are often softened by complicated language, omissions and evasions. Nobody who works in the organization volunteers to tell the boss that he or she is at the root of its difficulties.

Less excusably, peers from other, similar organizations who have been invited to make an independent assessment, or consultants who have been commissioned to do so, also seldom jump this final hurdle successfully. Peer evaluation frequently suffers from the fact that it is planned to be conducted mutually and that an unspoken deal is struck which compromises independence and robustness: 'If you scratch my back, I'll scratch yours.' There is an implied threat that too severe an answer to the question 'why?' will result in a similar battering when the questioner's own turn for scrutiny comes round. Some consultants, unfortunately, take the view that they are paid for saying what their client wants to hear. If that client is the root of many of an organization's ills, it might seem prudent to find ways to avoid saying so.

'And why?', therefore, are the hardest words in the Quality Assessment Framework. Only those who really do want or need to be world-class answer them. They are the test of the will to be outstanding.

In this chapter we have shown that consistent and reliable judgement about the quality of something as intensely human as learning is bound to be difficult. Those who do it will always be open to the accusation that their conclusions are merely subjective. Our strong conviction is that it is wrong to default on that account to a narrowly defined set of rules, compliance with which can less controversially be measured. Our reasoning is that world-class performance cannot be prescribed. It is the result of the endeavour, creativity and effectiveness of every individual, gathered together by sensitive and supportive managers. Their combined effect on learning can reliably be judged by referring to a framework and insisting that evidence used in answering the questions it poses is rigorously tested by triangulation and debate.

We need to assess the value of learning to help its further improvement, not to constrain it in the interest of measurement. We deplore the cynicism of the saying 'what gets measured gets done'. All too often what gets measured gets crushed. Assessment and assessors must be accurate, but they must also be humane.

Case Study 2

BMW Group UK Ltd: striving for consistent excellence

BMW is one of the world's leading manufacturers of premium cars. Based in Munich in Germany, it has an extensive dealer network in Britain, providing marketing, sales and service. This has been built up since the 1970s. The present British company, BMW Group UK Limited, was formed in 1981 and distributes cars and parts to its 148 dealers across the country. Apart from BMW cars themselves, the BMW dealer network is the most potent representative of the BMW brand with which British customers come into contact. A bad experience with a salesperson, or while a BMW is being serviced or repaired, damages the reputation of the company as certainly as would a faulty vehicle.

Consistently high performance over time depends heavily on the success of the BMW Group UK training programme. Technicians, sales staff and managers are trained not only to establish their primary professional skills through an apprenticeship but repeatedly to enhance those skills through the company's four levels of Certified, Professional, Expert and Master. They also learn to adapt them to successive generations of BMWs. The company receives a British government subsidy of about £1.5 million a year to help meet apprentice training costs.

BMW's apprentice training was first inspected by the ALI in 2002. Its management of training was given a grade 4: 'unsatisfactory'. This judgement depended largely on evidence that apprentice training was only loosely quality assured and varied widely across the country. BMW was aware that standards varied from one dealership to another, potentially damaging the company's reputation for premium quality associated with 'the ultimate driving machine'.

BMW training was contracted out at that time to five public, further education colleges. Some were good; some less so. Variation was, itself, contrary to the company's interest. Too little had been done to manage and reduce it by, for example, imposing tight performance conditions on the colleges and monitoring their fulfilment closely.

The company's response to the inspection report, which appeared on the internet and which was harmful to its reputation, was to accept promptly that it had a problem and to act. It took all its service apprentice training in-house.

Today, that training is delivered at the new, £17 million 'BMW Group Academy UK', built in the middle of a championship golf course near Reading, England. At a further ALI inspection in 2004, BMW was awarded grade 1 (outstanding) for both its leadership and management and its training programme in engineering, technology and manufacturing. It sets, and exceeds, measurable performance targets for itself. These include the number of training days (46,000 training days for UK dealers); year-on-year reduction of staff turnover, which is traditionally high in the motor industry and in which every 1 per cent reduction is worth £1.6 million to BMW; maximum efficiency in the use of training facilities, which exceeds the BMW company target by 40 per cent; and a gradual increase in the proportion of electronic independent learning from 10 per cent of total learning hours in 2006 to 25 per cent in 2010.

The company has also been given independent praise for its training provision. This includes a 'National Training Award', the 'Employer of the Year' award from the UK government funding body for training; a 'Learning and Skills Beacon' award from the British government; the Top Training BMW Group subsidiary in the company worldwide; and winning the top two places in a competition for BMW service technicians among nearly 12,000 employed in 33 countries.

BMW Group UK openly attributes the success of its apprentice training programme, and the rapid and accurately-targeted changes it made to achieve it, to its ALI inspection.

3

Using the Framework

Matching something apparently as dry as a written framework with what real people do requires a leap of imagination. You could see the sequence of experiences, revelations, insights, disappointments and triumphs, which is inseparable from learning new things, as a journey. The chart shown in Figure 3.1 is adapted from *Learner-centred Self-Assessment* published by the ALI. It matches the steps usually found in good adult learning with questions 2–6 of the Quality Assessment Framework, set out in the previous chapter, but in a slightly different order. Question 2 of the Framework, about achievement, relates to steps near the end of The Learner's Journey. The reason for the shift is that the focus of the Framework is on outcomes. As we suggest in this chapter, all the careful induction, teaching and learner support in the world is of no use if learners do not succeed in what they set out to achieve. We need carefully to assess all the steps in The Learner's Journey, but to do so in the context of a destination intended and reached.

Where you see the learner's footprints, there it is likely that each question in the Framework will need to be asked, picturing it as related to a step in The Learner's Journey. For example, when we evaluate how well the first contact between a learner and a learning provider is managed – recruitment – we need to ask questions 4, 5 and 6 from the Framework. Are people taken in willy-nilly, because they represent income on the hoof? Or do managers organize a careful sequence of honest marketing, sensitive interviewing and objective guidance which results in the offer

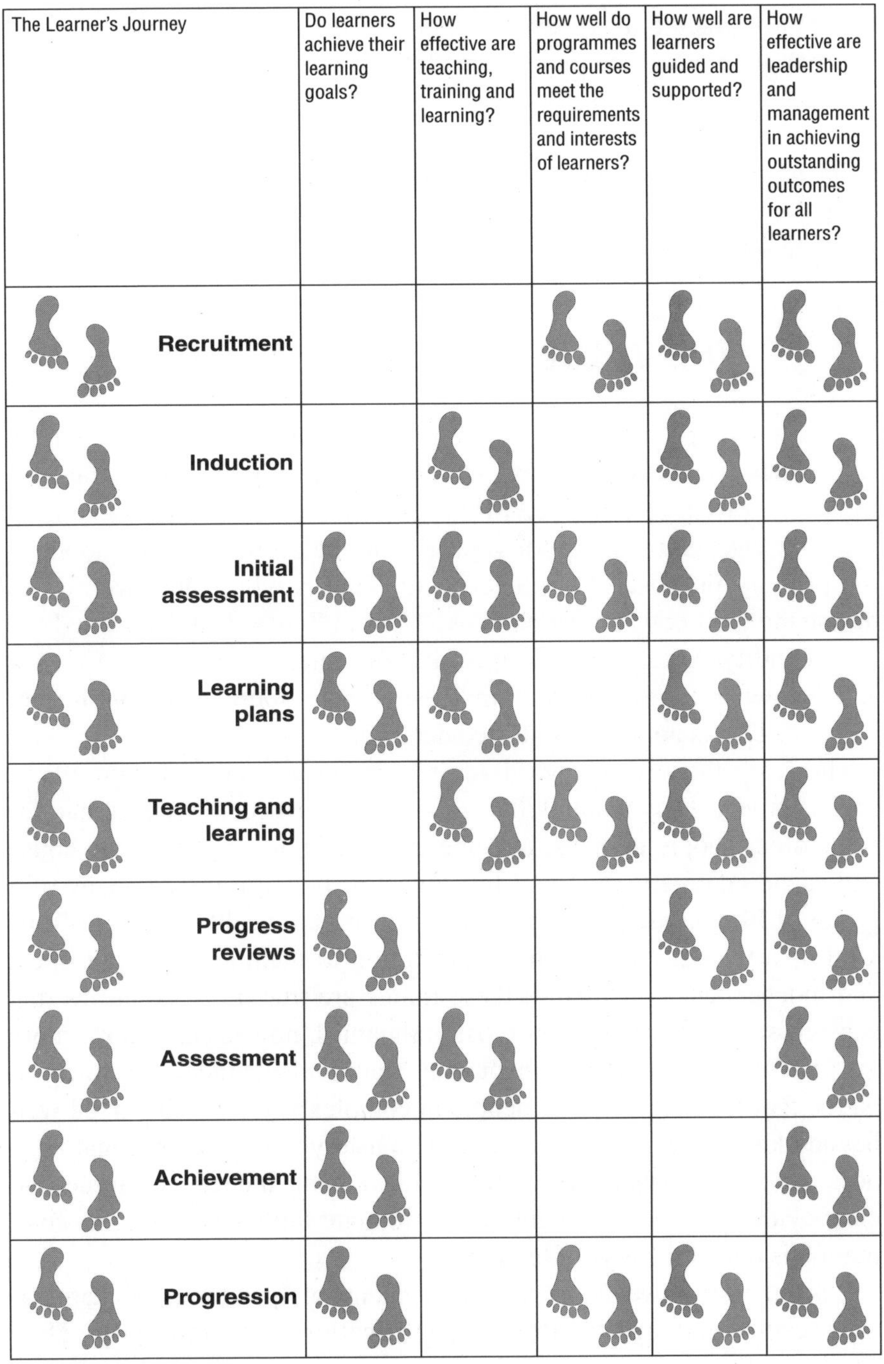

The Learner's Journey	Do learners achieve their learning goals?	How effective are teaching, training and learning?	How well do programmes and courses meet the requirements and interests of learners?	How well are learners guided and supported?	How effective are leadership and management in achieving outstanding outcomes for all learners?
Recruitment			👣	👣	👣
Induction		👣		👣	👣
Initial assessment	👣	👣	👣	👣	👣
Learning plans	👣	👣		👣	👣
Teaching and learning		👣	👣	👣	👣
Progress reviews	👣			👣	👣
Assessment	👣	👣			👣
Achievement	👣				👣
Progression	👣		👣	👣	👣

Figure 3.1 The Learner's Journey

of a study place only if the provider can be sure that it has the most appropriate programme for each candidate's needs?

Similarly, if we look down the list nearer the end of The Learner's Journey, at achievement once more, we can see that a favourable judgement on the work of the provider will be made only if managers have done the very best for each learner, resulting in their meeting or exceeding their own expectations.

THE VALUE OF QUALIFICATIONS

We are uncompromising in our conviction that people embark on the sometimes frightening, always challenging, business of learning new things in order to achieve. Moving to somewhere else; becoming someone else; doing better for yourself and the people you care about, is the primary purpose of adult learning. That is why, when we helped devise the *Common Inspection Framework* in England, and designed our own Quality Assessment Framework for international use, we took achievement out of its position in The Learner's Journey and put it right up front. That is not an uncontested decision.

There are those who regard adult learning as, very substantially, a social activity. They point, with a good deal of justice, to the fact that, for some older people perhaps, learning is a reason to get out of the house and spend an entertaining and fulfilling few hours in the company of a group of like-minded people. They point out the health benefits of this kind of learning, its powerful contribution to maintaining self-respect and independence. Whilst all these things are true, most countries that subsidize adult learning, and most companies, nowadays impose more instrumental tests of achievement when they evaluate their investment. It is true that learning enriches people in complex ways which extend well beyond knowledge acquisition and the mastery of subject, but that richness is not diminished by tangible achievement. Indeed, we argue that clear evidence of achievement helps stimulate further progress; its celebration is one of the joys of learning.

It is too easy, however, to see achievement solely in terms of examination results and qualifications. Qualifications are important. They emphatically confirm personal attainment and growing self-worth in ways which are often heart-warming to the teacher, as well as profession-ally satisfying and apparently precise. However, they seldom equate exactly with the real operational capability of individuals at work or the skills of a population which are relevant to succeeding in the global market. They are an indicator, and a useful one at that, but they are not the be-all and end-all. For that reason, while it is understandable that governments routinely set achievement targets in terms of the number, level, and even the type of qualifications won by their citizens each year, counting awards is only the beginning of a sound assessment of achieve-ment in a learning organization.

Ford Motor Company's Employee Development and Assistance Programme (EDAP) scheme famously offered employees the opportunity for subsidized study in any topic they wanted, reasoning that all learning is of value even if not immediately. Unipart, enlightened though it is in its approach to learning, pays only for study towards qualifications that help the bearer to make a greater contribution to the business. To satisfy the requirements of the Quality Assessment Framework, the real value of both these approaches needs to be understood, judged and justified.

The complexities around awards become still more acute when learn-ers fail to achieve them. Where learning takes place at work and someone is diverted from completing a qualification by promotion or a move to a better job, how is that to be judged? Do we castigate it as a qualification failed or praise it as the ultimate objective achieved? Is it the kind of 'outstanding outcome' we want managers to strain every sinew to help learners to reach?

This dilemma is seldom easily resolved. Those who take a hard line that qualifications must be achieved at all costs run the risk of being seen as out of touch with business realities, dwellers in an academic ivory tower. Those who too readily excuse dropping out from a course of study, on the other hand, risk selling the learner short. Studying alongside work and often in the evenings and at weekends can be tough. It is easy to drop out, especially for a 'good' reason. But what may look like the obviously sensible decision today, satisfying employee and employer alike, may not look such a good idea a few years hence, when 'failed' learners find themselves under-qualified for a new job elsewhere. Here the interests of the individual learner should come to the fore. It is rarely sensible to achieve most of what is needed to gain a qualification and not go for the award. Qualifications confer independence and choice in life on those who hold them – but may even be seen as working against the interests of the short-sighted business concerned to keep its staff.

Dealing properly with this issue requires mature judgement. If it is a frequent occurrence that learners spend time in state-subsidized study but do not achieve the award which would represent a long-term good for them and for their country, then it is deserving of condemnation. If an employer routinely withdraws its staff from learning as soon as they know enough or can do what is needed for immediate purposes, it is deserving of condemnation. If an employer routinely dismisses staff just before they complete their apprenticeships and qualify for higher pay – as we have seen too many times – it is deserving of condemnation. If early drop-out is unusual and it is invariably associated with identifiable and verifiable benefit to the individual, then it should be accepted as one of the normal attributes of adult, work-based learning.

Zealotry is rarely attractive. Even the suspicion of it needs to be guarded against in an area as sensitive as quality assessment. The Quality Assessment Framework, used to secure a sensible and pragmatic interpretation of evidence, should be proof against that. Fortunately, there is also a growing realization among employers, in our country at least, that investing in employees' learning does not encourage them to leave and work for a competitor which freeloads on the investment. Far from it. Paying for learning binds employees to the company which they rightly feel is showing a long-term interest in their development and career progression. That has proved true even in businesses like supermarket retailing, where an international giant like Tesco reports that training helps drastically reduce the retailer's nightmare: people who leave in their first year in the trade. Tesco's personnel manager is quoted as saying, 'A lot of our staff are building an emotional loyalty to Tesco. The benefits outweigh the risks.'[1]

MEASURING ADDED VALUE

The 'achievement' question also raises one of the trickiest problems in quality assessment – that of measuring added value. Anybody can credibly assert that disadvantaged people, with few or no previous qualifications, have received a real boost when they gain their first award. We have seen it happen many times. We have seen it in family learning, where parents and their children perhaps learn to read alongside one another; in prisons where people who typically have the literacy skills normal for a child of seven gain their first secondary-school-level qualification; in welfare-to-work programmes where people who have been long-term unemployed get their first decent job in years. One would have to be very cynical indeed to take part in these events dry-eyed.

But if quality assessment is to be helpful to such probably admirable organizations in guiding them to raise their game still further, we need some means of judging just how much value has been added to the learning experience by that organization. Almost certainly, for example, the experience itself of studying alongside other family members or with other people who share similar learning deficits would help people to progress. The organization being assessed may have done little more than bring these people together.

To separate clear judgement from instinctive support in such matters is seldom easy. In part, it can be achieved by evaluating the learning journey. Do we know, can we be shown clearly, where each learner started? Was a thorough initial assessment made of their capabilities, perhaps using psychometric tests, structured interviews to tease out the skills learnt at work and in daily life, or tests of competency? Was an appropriate programme of study chosen, which would stretch their apparent abilities without leaving them floundering, and was it adjusted as a result of regular further assessments of their growing abilities? Evidence like this of a systematic approach to measuring progress can offer reassurance that instinctive celebration of blossoming ability is not blinding the assessor's eye to the organizational contribution. It will also, almost certainly, show up things that could be done better.

At the individual level, or the level of relatively small groups of individuals, this kind of evaluation will probably suffice to assure the assessor that worthwhile things are happening.

Where there is a national ladder of formal, probably academic awards, like the English school qualifications normally taken at age 16 (GCSE) and age 18 (GCE A level), it is also fairly straightforward to devise a wider measure of added value. What is needed first is an average relationship between points scored in the GCSE examination and the

GCE A level, based on a sufficiently large sample of pupils, either within an individual school or college, a district or the country as a whole. Having determined average performance, it is easy to see whether each pupil or group of pupils – and by inference the institution in which they are taught – has done better or worse than might have been expected.

A particularly sophisticated version of this, developed and used by Greenhead College in the north of England, enables each new student at 16 to be told what is expected of them in the GCE A-level examination, two years hence. Experience has proved this to be a powerful motivator to young people, helping them perform better than predicted and so driving a virtuous circle of ever-rising results. The effect is further accentuated by the fact that teachers are also appraised according to whether the young people they have taught achieve better or worse than anticipated. In essence, this approach is similar to that of a national value-added measure (VA).

More complex is a similar requirement applied to competency-based vocational awards which may well not be graded, so that points are difficult to ascribe to performance, and where succeeding awards on a ladder of qualifications may be less easily compared than, for example, physics or mathematics at different stages of mastery. It can be done and is often described as 'distance travelled' (DT).

The difficulties arise partly, of course, from the fact that every adult is the sum of a mass of earlier knowledge and experience, most of which has nothing to do with formal learning and qualifications. David Sherlock once worked for a highly accomplished college principal who delighted in the double meaning in his description of his own learning journey as 'an unqualified success'. Like many other young men of his generation, any hope of attending university had been plucked away by conscription into the British Army to take part in the Second World War. As a conscientious objector he served as a medical orderly in the Parachute Regiment, taking part in the crossing of the Rhine and the liberation of the Belsen concentration camp. He then went on to Palestine, where he met his Israeli wife-to-be through the boundary wire of a military base. How do you put a points value on all that, comparable, let us say, with qualification for a university degree?

It is obviously foolish to try. But that wealth of experience, and mixing with other budding young artists in the Army, was what enabled the man to quickly learn a sculptor's skills and to make rich and interesting creative work. He was, in fact, an extraordinarily qualified success.

In that case, and in a host of others which, in the different circumstances of today nevertheless share some of its characteristics, it is still possible to distinguish between the impacts of life-skills, experience and technical instruction. But to do it fairly does call for sophistication. That sophistication comes from experience and from the use of evidence collected and weighed in a properly disciplined manner.

This really becomes important when it critically affects the overall judgement on a provider's capability. It is also very important as far as adult learners are concerned, when decisions are made about the level at which they should start learning a completely new professional discipline and the rate at which they should progress.

For example, when the Rover car company, based at Birmingham in the English Midlands, collapsed in 2005, over 6,000 people were abruptly dropped into the job market without the right skills set for the work available. Making accurate appraisals of what they, in fact, already knew and could do – rather than what qualifications they held – was critical in designing efficient retraining programmes for them. The care with which that was done, and the success of the end-result – good new jobs – would have been the means by which the 'distance travelled' credited to the training organizations that did the work could be judged.

That is what basing our definition of what is good, as far as learning providers are concerned, on what they help individual learners achieve means in practice. It helps us make sense of the apparent turmoil of everyday life and learning, in a way sharp enough to guide the improvement of learning organizations.

EFFECTIVE LEARNING

The next section of the Quality Assessment Framework, question 3, dealing with the effectiveness of teaching, training and learning, goes to the heart of the matter. There is often a marked difference between the apparent quality of teaching and the extent of learning that results. That we will deal with in Chapter 4. However, we should note here that there is a preferred model of teaching and learning implicit in the Framework.

In England, certainly, there is a lively debate, often conducted on very flimsy grounds, about the relative merits of 'formal' or 'traditional' teaching and 'informal' teaching. The former is generally held to mean that an authoritative teacher addresses a whole class, while the latter conveys the picture of teacher-as-facilitator, endeavouring to treat each and every learner according to their needs at that moment. In TVET, opportunities for whole-class, formal teaching do exist but they are usually few and far between. In work-based learning there are seldom any classes to attend. As we have discussed, the backgrounds of adults often vary so widely that some form of personalized approach to guiding and stimulating their learning has to be adopted.

It is these circumstances we have in mind in question 3 of the Framework. They are difficult to manage effectively.

A lot of responsibility for managing them in adult learning properly belongs with learners themselves. Building and harnessing the capacity of adult learners to motivate themselves, plan their own work to fit round their lives and study on their own is an important part of the teacher's job. Any simple notion that one pedagogy might be preferable to all others in a case like this is absurd.

So the Framework has to guide incisive professional debate about the merits of a wide range of different approaches to learning. But flexibility does not mean laxity. The 'indicators to inform the answer to this question' are deliberately phrased to be hard to slip away from. They aim to help you nail firmly whether the person leading learning has chosen the best circumstances to make it go well; how carefully progress is being assessed; how promptly problems are sorted out; how well fitted for the job that learning leader is and how methodically they do it; how creative they are in making sure every learner is able to give of their best. These are the key issues, whether we are looking at a formal lesson in a college, a workshop session, a programme of computer-based independent study followed at home or at the office desk, or learning on the job with guidance from a work supervisor and a visiting tutor and assessor.

EQUALITY AND DIVERSITY

The final 'indicator' in question 3 is, for us, very important. We recognize that it needs interpretation to meet the mores of different cultures. Two hundred years ago, the Emperor Napoleon, immersed in root-and-branch reform of the law and institutions of his country in the wake of the French Revolution, considered the nature of education. He concluded that equality of opportunity was fundamental to education; its kernel. Unless any system of learning gives everyone an equal opportunity to reach the limit of their potential, it is falling down on the job. He was hammering out this view at a time when, in our country for example, women, followers of any religion other than Anglican Christianity and anyone other than the wealthy were barred from university and the public school system was rudimentary.

This book makes a strong case, based on examples, that the productivity necessary to be a winner in the globalized world depends as much on getting 80 per cent or so of your working-age people into work as it does on ensuring that everything encourages maximum efficiency when they get there. That cannot be done if substantial sections of the population are denied access to the learning that would prepare them for work, and to the workplace itself.

An example from Britain: people from most minority ethnic communities in our country are poorer than their white fellow-citizens. Some of the poorest came originally from the agricultural Sylhet region of Bangladesh. According to a recent study, some 60 per cent of them, concentrated in the east end of London, live below the UK poverty line. They suffer from poor inner-city schooling and the lack of a tradition of learning in the home. And they suffer from the cultural inhibition that keeps most adult women at home and away from work. Some of the inequality of opportunity suffered by this minority community is undoubtedly imposed by a state whose learning provision is largely geared to the needs of the majority, but some of it is voluntary; a matter of choice.

We would not wish to challenge the right to that choice, in this country or in others. But we point out that it has significant consequences. Our concern for equality of opportunity is principled. It derives from the democratic secular tradition from which we grew. But it is also pragmatic; it is the most efficient way of doing things.

Much the same needs to be said about the value of diversity. This is not crass 'political correctness'. It is the result of observation that teams made up from people with different attitudes, skills and abilities cover all the bases. They are rarely caught out by unforeseen difficulties. You would not want a company board made up entirely of 45-year-old, white, male accountants, because they would lack the skills to do some of the things the organization needs to thrive. They might well miss some of the business opportunities offered by serving the other 50 per cent of the human race and they would all retire at the same time, leaving the company leaderless. Prudent organizations include a range of professional background, gender, age and temperament among their top executives. The same argument has force in all walks of life.

The Framework suggests that, to get real benefit from diversity, positive adjustments have to be made. We have worked with the British armed services, helping them recover from earlier bad advice to the effect that equal opportunities legislation required that all recruits be treated exactly the same. Some years earlier, recognizing that modern warfare is no longer a matter of deploying human physical strength, the armed forces had started to recruit women in significant numbers, to work and fight alongside men. However, misconception about their legal obligations led the forces to abandon a policy called 'Gender Fair' in favour of 'Gender Free'. Young women had to be able to march 30 kilometres, carrying a 25kg pack, as well as young men. The result was an epidemic of stress fractures in the lower limbs and pelvises of young women. Accommodations – often more subtle than in this case – have to be made to secure real equality of opportunity and real benefit from diversity among learners. The economic benefits in a globalized economy are well worth it.

MATCHING LEARNING TO LEARNERS

Question 4 of the Framework is about the appropriateness of the opportunity offered. At the simple level, this means avoiding putting people on courses that they are bound to fail, or on ones that will give them little benefit for the longer term.

Obvious though it may be, governments and learning organizations often fall straight into this trap. Britain has a tradition of apprenticeship going back 500 years or more. Young people were 'bound' to a master craftsman for a set period of years and learnt a trade until they achieved 'journeyman' status. This structure lasted until the 1980s when it was increasingly recognized that some people were able to progress faster than others and that not all skills in the modern world took five years to acquire. In the early 1990s 'Modern Apprenticeships' were launched, using the competency-based National Vocational Qualification (see our Introduction) as their core.

Much as apprenticeships had once been, Modern Apprenticeships were aimed at 16-year-old school leavers and were seen as broadly comparable in the demand they made with the GCE A-level exam others in the peer group were taking in order to qualify for university. All well and good one might think – except that in a number of professional disciplines, only one in four or five modern apprentices achieved the award they wanted.

A primary reason for this was that too few of them had done well enough in the GCSE examinations, which are the entry qualification for study – academic or its vocational equivalents – at GCE A level. They had no realistic prospect of doing well and they should never have been allowed to start a Modern Apprenticeship. But there was no alternative. Not until the British government began to build a ladder of apprenticeship curricula and awards, with entry points suited to different levels of prior attainment, did the results and outcomes for learners start to get better.

Now the apprenticeship ladder of qualifications begins on the lowest rung with Entry to Employment (E2E) for young people who have effectively dropped out of schooling sometime between the ages of 11 and 16 and have no qualifications; Apprenticeship for 16-year-olds without the necessary GCSE levels; Advanced Apprenticeship, the original GCSE A-level equivalent, now open only to those qualified to enter; and a Foundation Degree, allowing study at work that could count towards a university honours degree.

This may well be an extreme example of the old saying that 'The road to Hell is paved with good intentions.' Traditional time-served apprenticeships were long enough and ill-defined enough to take the rough with the smooth as far as the ability of apprentices was concerned. Rude comments about apprentices abound in English literature. We can be pretty sure that a good many had to have their rough edges knocked off by growing up and coming to terms gradually with adult life and work. The trouble was that the more able and enthusiastic paid the price by being locked into apprenticeship much longer than they needed. Taking out this injustice with Modern Apprenticeship also unwittingly took out the flexibility to deal effectively with the weaker or more obstreperous youngsters. The law of unintended consequences came down with a vengeance, to punish all concerned.

The point is that programmes of learning need to pass the Goldilocks test. They must not be too easy for the learner concerned, or too hard. They must be just right. It must be possible to adapt them to new advances in technology and new demands from the fast-moving world of work in a globalized economy. There need to be enough choices to match the reasonable demands of adults fitting in learning alongside earning a living and raising a family. And there should not be unnecessary barriers placed in the way of further advancement for those who open up new horizons through learning.

One last concern: work-based learning, where study is split in various proportions between learning through on-the-job instruction and experience, and off-the-job acquisition of knowledge and theory, is inherently hard to organize. At its best, it is uniquely effective, because new knowledge and its practical application are closely aligned. It ensures that people use all their faculties – hearing, sight, touch; doing as well as being told – to make sure that lessons are thoroughly grasped and can be built on securely. That ideal is sometimes badly missed. There is little or no coordination between theory and practice. Learners are told something new but fail to take it seriously because it seems irrelevant, only to find some time later that it was fundamental to dealing with a practical matter at work.

Even colleges where students visit several campuses in the course of study sometimes get things horribly wrong by failing to coordinate different elements of learning. One set of staff goes about its teaching in complete isolation from the next. They move forward at different rates. Tests are set in one place that could only be successfully taken if a lesson due the following week at another campus had happened earlier. Learners are left to make sense of what might once have been a coherent syllabus but is now a hodgepodge of unrelated facts.

The Framework requires that a quality assessor checks this out. Once again, evidence will be built up by checking the syllabus against individual lesson plans, students' opinions and their workbooks, all contextualized by what teachers and managers have to say about it. We have heard teachers say, 'Oh, it does them good to puzzle it out and make connections on their own.' We were not convinced.

SUPPORT FOR LEARNING

The fifth question in the Framework deals with the vexed question of adult guidance. It is vexed among some guidance professionals because they have a concern that adults should always be free to make up their own minds. This is true. Few adults relish being told what to do. However, learning is an insecure business, involving journeys into the unknown which are sometimes not only intellectually discomforting but also potentially disruptive of families and careers. Learners need help. The more inexperienced or out of practice they are at learning, the more help they are likely to need.

That is what this question prompts you to tease out. Are learners being given enough help, not only to study successfully but often also to find ways of fitting in study alongside other important things? Are they being shoe-horned into courses for the convenience of the provider, perhaps because a particular programme is under-subscribed or particularly profitable, rather than those that fit their own requirements? Impartial guidance might extend to recommending a different provider and helping the learner to transfer. Is there readily available access to specialist professional help for people for whom learning has proved terribly destabilizing, perhaps causing psychological disturbance or confirming marriage breakdown or challenging religious convictions?

Education and training is not a branch of the social services. Nevertheless, we have seen over the years how subversive of once-held certainties all learning, any learning in any subject, can be. Learning is supposed to be life-changing (we hope life-enhancing) and providers have an obligation, we suggest, to offer easy access to professionals who can help pick up the pieces when the change goes much further than was imagined.

Let us come down to a slightly less uncomfortable level to illustrate the kind of role good learning support can play, attracting favourable comment under the Framework. A college we knew well in southern England had a serious problem with student absenteeism. Lessons often lost momentum because students arrived late or turned up only occasionally and time had to be spent helping them catch up with what they had missed. Seeing a minority indulged and compensated for learning they, themselves, had caused to be missed, more and more students became casual about punctuality and attendance.

Gradual corrosion of the institution's effectiveness by its own learners clearly needed firm and comprehensive action right across the college. A system was introduced through which teachers notified the student services unit of absences within five minutes of the start of learning sessions, using electronic pagers. The student services staff would then telephone the homes of absentees, immediately, within an hour or so of the start of the morning, afternoon or evening sessions. If they got a reply, they would ask the learner or their families whether they were all right: were they unwell? If there was no reply, they would visit the house, the same day, either speaking to the learner or family members, or leaving a note expressing anxiety for the learner's welfare.

The results were dramatic. Absenteeism and lateness dropped sharply. Contrary to many expectations, the new procedure was not resented as an intrusion into private life, but welcomed as a clear sign that the college cared deeply about its learners. Outstanding learner support is, we emphasize once again, about securing maximum benefit for each and every individual learner. Its presence can often be seen, if you will pardon the apparent contradiction, in the consistency with which extraordinary steps are taken to make adult learning possible.

ASSESSING LEADERSHIP

Leadership and management must be the most thoroughly explored topics on the planet. We can think of few others which are subject to the attentions of so-called 'gurus'. No other area of the Framework is likely to tempt people towards the lazy thought that a judgement about the quality of leadership might be used as a proxy for judgement about a whole learning organization. We are profoundly opposed to this. We believe it to be a bad mistake which should have been consigned to the waste bin along with pre-Tolstoyan military history, which once mistakenly assumed that the story of the Macedonian conquest of Persia was just about the personal doings of Alexander the Great. Just as modern military history is a sophisticated blend of evaluating plans, the decisions of generals and their subordinate commanders, the influence of the battlefield, the experiences of individual combatants and the political environment in which the whole affair took place, so modern analysis of the effectiveness of organizations – including learning organizations – has to be multi-factorial.

The phrasing of question 6 has been chosen with particular care. We happily acknowledge our debt to Jim Collins and his perceptive analysis of leading the transition from 'Good to Great'.[2] Effective leaders, at all levels of organizations, undoubtedly have a critical role to play in defining what needs to be done and getting it done efficiently. These things are described in the 'indicators'. What we also want to emphasize is that the people for whom they are done are learners.

In using the Framework, we are not interested in qualities of leadership and management for their own sake. We would be profoundly disturbed if people assessing the quality of leadership and management in a learning organization praised or lambasted it solely according to whether it conformed to any of the gurus' recommendations or the recognized standards. There is no room in assessing learning quality for people who bring their own preconceptions to the business, who see it as an opportunity to ride their own hobby-horses. What we are seeking, here, is an evidence-based judgement of whether or not the actions of people exercising leadership and management produce the optimum outcome, the outstanding outcome in the globalized world, for learners. That is why almost every one of the 'indicators' pegs the issue back to the kind of benefits that learners might be expected to receive if it were done well.

One of the outcomes of our work in inspectorates over the past 14 years, which often distressed us, was the tendency of governing bodies or boards to fire the boss if the judgements we made about their organization were severe. The dismissal was sometimes justified, although we seldom saw any good reason why the rest of the board should not fall on its swords as well. But very often it was simply a knee-jerk reaction, based on the kind of simplistic attribution of every good or bad result to the person at the top, which we criticized when first addressing question 6. As Jim Collins points out, in social sector organizations, into which category many involved in learning fall, the person at the top sets the tasks, the aspirations and the tone, but rarely has direct executive control. Power is often distributed and therefore judgements about the effectiveness of leadership and management in securing outstanding outcomes for learners need to be carefully targeted on the part of the organization where they rightfully belong. We have encountered excellent organizations, from the learners' point of view, where the chief executive was morally or ethically repugnant, or wholly inept. Equally, we have had to tell fine, able people that their fears that they were presiding over a disaster were justified and that they were doing the wrong things to pull the situation back. Some organizations, too, are beyond help.

What the notion of distributed responsibility for exercising leadership and management skills implies is the existence of secure performance management at every level. Our view is that learning organizations must arrange for teachers to be regularly observed at work in the classroom or workshop by their managers. Similarly, these managers' performance and achievements should be appraised, and so on to the top, including the members of any governing board. It is unimportant, in a social-sector organization, whether those who operate in it are unpaid volunteers, part-time workers or salaried professionals. Their commitment is to an outstanding outcome for every learner and it is reasonable that the effectiveness of their contributions should be formally managed. It would be surprising, would it not, if the people who ran a learning organization did not also follow The Learner's Journey, with its requirement for establishing what they can do now and what they need to do soon, for the benefit of all concerned?

GRADING

One last thing needs to be covered in this chapter. You will recall from our Introduction that one of the innovations of 1993 in England was attribution of numerical grades to summarize the quality of each particular element of the Framework. We supported it then and nothing has come along since to change our minds.

The grading scale we have arrived at by a process of elimination and refinement is this:

Grade 1   Outstanding
Grade 2   Good
Grade 3   Satisfactory
Grade 4   Inadequate

The fact that there is an even number of grades prevents the idle default to the mid-point which tends to happen with three-point, five-point or seven-point scales. The use of a numerical scale forces assessors to make up their minds about the quality of provision. It stops them falling back on the kind of ambiguous words that will probably leave the organization puzzled about what the assessors thought at the time, and totally bewildered about what it should do a few months later. Numerical grades can be tracked over time, showing clearly whether a teacher, a department, a learning provider or an entire national system is improving or falling behind. The fact that there are three above-the-line grades in our four-point scale allowed us, in the ALI, to give a gold award for an overall grade 1; a silver for grade 2; and a bronze for grade 3. Grade 4 got nothing at all, except help to improve. More of that later. Our experience is that every organization wants a 'gold award' in its reception area. The majority who get silver or bronze will work hard for their learners to get gold next time.

On the face of it, then, numerical grades have everything going for them: they head off lazy assessors; they avoid ambiguity; they support providers' aspiration to be outstanding; and they illustrate rising and falling trends over time. We are convinced these advantages are compelling and that any organization or nation wanting to be a serious player in the globalized economy should quickly overcome any scruples it may have about using them.

The Quality Assessment Framework is short and apparently simple. In delving beneath its surface in this chapter we hope not to have left you with an impression that assessing learning is impossibly complicated but, rather, that every question is susceptible to sophisticated debate. The *Common Inspection Framework* in England has been an overwhelming success because every teacher, every instructor, every learning provider can recognize something of their own practice in it. It draws people in because it is simple. What must be avoided is its simplistic application.

Case Study 3

West Berkshire Adult Community Learning: responsiveness versus quality

Adult community learning seeks to meet the wishes and needs of mature people who invariably study for just a few hours each week. It involves about 1 million learners in England, many of them women and many retired from full-time work. A lot of people start courses for recreation, studying initially at least for personal interest, even though some of them go on to use their new knowledge or skills as the basis for fresh jobs or businesses. There are many innovative programmes which draw together different generations of families or groups of friends or work colleagues, particularly in basic literacy and numeracy or information and communications technology (ICT). A part of the social fabric of local communities, these courses are often organized by local government but taught in schools, libraries, church halls and even people's homes to make them easily accessible. Programme organizers often work through an extended network of agencies, many of them voluntary, over which they have little control.

In 2003, the ALI found the courses provided for nearly 10,000 people by West Berkshire local education authority inadequate. A number of important areas of learning were awarded grade 4, including ICT; hospitality, sport, leisure and travel; and English, languages and communication. The leadership and management of the programme – a multiplicity of courses taught by a further education college, a community school and several charities – was also awarded grade 4. Community learning, the provider's avowed 'jewel in the crown', was confirmed as being good, even though it was available in over 50 local centres. While geographical dispersal and delegated delivery were problems with much of the provision, they were evidently not insurmountable.

West Berkshire's nominee said of this first ALI inspection, 'It brought everybody up short, but it was a tremendous lever. It gave us the influence to insist on changes.' All the delivery partners came together in a provider group to explore their shortcomings and agree remedies. Open debate within the framework set by the inspection report and the strong public service values of the team created 'an ethos of trust. Discussions that might otherwise have been uncomfortable – about weaknesses in teaching for example – were much easier.' They had confidence in the inspector leading the re-inspection: 'we were very clear about what was expected of us and what was going to happen'. A strong focus on finding evidence to support or eliminate assumptions grew up in the group, under the impetus of preparing for re-inspection. 'Without evidence, good practice becomes invisible and poor practice can be condoned.'

When re-inspection was complete in 2004, great improvements were confirmed. The weak areas of learning – the principal concern of learners themselves – were all re-graded as good; grade 2. However, leadership and management, while better than before, were still just satisfactory. The nominee thought deeply about this result and said, 'Where I have come to is that leadership and management are not just about what the senior management team and I do. They are a whole team effort. It's about how persuaded our partners are and what they do as a result in terms of planning, quality assurance and training for tutors.'

By 2007, West Berkshire Adult Community Learning had mastered this distributed form of leadership. At a fresh inspection, leadership and management and the overall effectiveness of the provider were locked together: both at grade 2. 'The important thing is making a difference to people's lives. To do that you have absolutely got to have a consistent standard of quality. That's one message inspection drove home: the importance of consistency.'

Notes

1   Kingston, P (2007) 'In-house training goes national', *The Guardian* newspaper, UK, 1 May
2   Collins, J (2001) *Good to Great*, Random House, Business Books, London
     Collins, J (2006) *Good to Great and the Social Sectors*, Random House, Business Books, London

4

How to judge learning

Ask almost anyone who has achieved success and they will give you the name of the teacher who struck the first spark. It may have been the beginning of a lifelong enthusiasm for a subject. As often as not, it had little or nothing to do with what was taught but everything to do with the way it was taught. To have your potential believed in by someone you admire is often enough to launch a lifetime's career and lifelong learning.

And yet the Unipart experience (Case Study 1) reminds us of something we all know. Traditional teaching, using formal instruction to fill supposedly empty vessels with knowledge organized by someone else, is often very ineffective. Unipart call it 'pour and snore'. Sitting still while someone reads from a textbook, or talks to a whiteboard on which they write supposedly illuminating notes, can be as dull as ditchwater. Superficially, the teacher may give the performance of a lifetime but, very often, nothing is learnt.

Avoiding such a sterile dialogue lies at the heart of any realistic process for improving the quality of learning. Learning that is retained, learning that transforms lives, is a process of personal discovery. It is a flash of understanding or insight. It is the satisfying click when a host of small lessons coheres into new knowledge. It does not have to involve a qualified teacher, and often, as far as experienced adult learners are concerned, it does not. The instrument of change and progress for them is as likely to be a workmate showing how to do something new, or a debate with others, or a package of information on the internet. But at least for those many people newly drawn into lifelong learning by the demands of globalization, an effective informal or formal transaction with a teacher of some kind is likely to be needed sometime.

We use the word 'teacher' very broadly. We mean it to include technical instructors, demonstrators, supervisors and mentors at work. We mean it to include anyone who regularly works to help other people learn. For adults, it implies a relationship of respect, but preferably not one of authority. Ideally, their relationship entails enjoyment.

Figure 4.1 shows just how uneven effective learning is in Britain, across the various levels and age groups. The top bar shows the stages of learning, from elementary schooling through to learning at work and at university. The lower bar shows England's ranking among 30 countries surveyed by the OECD. We do well at either end, among the very young and the academic high-fliers at university. We serve very badly the lower achievers, those who leave school early, those fighting to catch up with lost opportunities or the new demands of the global economy by learning at work. There is, in Britain, a persistent 'tail' of underachievers, amounting to around a fifth of every group of school leavers, who will always struggle to keep up with the new demands.

In a seminal report *A Fresh Start*[1] by a former government statistician, Lord Claus Moser, Britain was confronted with the unwelcome news that about one adult in every five has difficulty with the level of literacy now

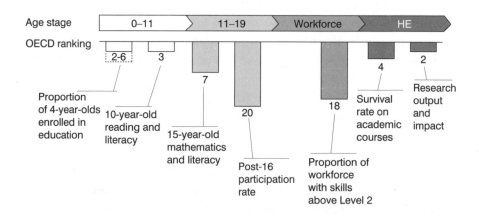

Figure 4.1   Performance of the English education system
Source: Department of Education and Skills, UK

required to get and hold a rewarding job, and even more, about one in four, always contend with the essentials of numeracy.

There is only one fair conclusion. It is that, while it is reasonably straightforward to find sufficient teachers able to do a good job with people who are easy to teach – the very young, the very intelligent – it is much more difficult to meet the needs of people who most need to learn in their own best interests, but who are unable or unwilling to do so. This group includes rebellious adolescents, people who find school or college dull and adults who can just get by without learning new things. Striking that first spark for them, perhaps at an advanced age, can be very hard indeed. Teachers who do it, mainly to be found in the TVET systems of the world, need help and support to succeed.

IT HELPS TO BE WATCHED

In many countries, notions of professional autonomy prevent TVET teachers from getting that help. Trades unions and professional associations – wrongly, we suggest – often argue that the teacher's classroom or lecture theatre or workshop is their private domain. They argue that respect for the teacher's professionalism demands that they be left alone with their learners year after year, without the presence or intervention of anyone else, least of all a manager concerned with assessing and improving performance. This attitude is not simply dog-in-the-manger exclusivity on the part of teachers. It is found among many professions that involve doing things with or to other people.

It is, however, a position that is crumbling steadily the world over. There was a time when commercial airline pilots would not question or intervene in each other's actions, however catastrophic. That time ended in Britain with a fatal accident at Heathrow Airport when the first officer failed forcibly to take over the controls from a captain who was suffering a heart attack. There was a time when community data on deaths were not monitored and analysed closely. That time ended in Britain when a doctor was convicted of murdering 15 elderly patients and was alleged to have killed over 200 before anyone became sufficiently anxious to intervene.

The damage done by ineffective teachers who are allowed to persist in their ineffectiveness is less dramatic than this. However, they can cause real harm; a lifetime's underachievement among those they were supposed to help.

This chapter continues our coverage of Assessment, one of the cardinal facets of The Transformational Diamond. The unique offering of our method of quality improvement, the skill derived from nearly 200 years of inspection in England, is observation and accurate analysis of the teacher at work; the learning process itself. Let us re-emphasize a key point. Observation is not about nit-picking. It is not a process of personal criticism or humiliation. It is a means for identifying what is strong and what is weak in the performance of a teacher, on a single occasion or a handful, in promoting learning. Its purpose is to help teachers to be more effective and take greater satisfaction from what they do, so that learners gain more from a central, precious transaction in the process of adult learning.

Certainly, we have observed some very bad teaching in the past 14 years, but not much of it. What we have seen a great deal more often are magical sessions of learning in which the teacher is almost wholly unconscious of how extraordinary they are. We have seen teachers on the edge of tears when we told them, privately after an observed lesson, that what they had done was outstandingly good. 'I've been teaching for 26 years. Nobody has ever told me that! Nobody has ever come into one of my lessons' was a typical response from one of these, a maths lecturer in a large college. There is no threat to teachers' professional status from observing and commenting on their work in order to help them improve – provided the job is done well.

Observation may be part of a self-assessment process, about which more later. It may be part of a mutually agreed peer-review process, or it may be at the heart of independent assessment by an official agency such as an inspectorate. In any case, whether the process is set in motion by the learning organization itself or is imposed upon it by law or contract, it is essential to build understanding and consensus.

PREPARING TO SHINE

We have conducted inspections of some military installations and some prisons without notice. We did so with the short-term intention of re-establishing public confidence. We were saying, in effect, 'We tried to catch them out but could not.' Everybody involved understood that. The much more complex long-term investment in building a continuous improvement culture came later, when normality had been restored.

There is also a body of opinion in England that inspecting with very little notice is the right thing to do. According to this argument, the arrival of inspectors causes so much stress among teachers that it is better that they cannot suffer it through anticipation of independent assessment during a lengthy notice period. It is also argued that the provider will be more nearly in its everyday unembellished state if it is visited at short notice. We know of little or no evidence to support the first of these propositions. How can it be less anxious for staff to expect the sudden irruption of strangers any time in the year when they are 'due' in an inspection cycle, than on a specified and agreed date some months hence? So far as achieving certainty that external assessors will encounter normality in a provider is concerned, there are many stories, true or apocryphal, to suggest that sometimes they do not. If an atmosphere of antagonism builds up, human beings in any country and from any culture will pull the wool over the eyes of those in authority. The British are masters at it. Fortunately, however, these concerns are largely irrelevant if observation is firmly linked to quality improvement.

What you do during a lengthy notice period is significant. With the ALI it began with a letter to the provider, informing it that it had been selected for inspection. A copy of the very handsomely produced inspection toolkit went as well, with its first section devoted to a careful explanation of how the selection had taken place. It invited providers for which the date chosen was inappropriate to make a case for deferral. A deferred inspection was obviously sensible and justified where the provider would have no learners at the time chosen, for example, but it was unlikely to be granted for the host of more frivolous reasons against which experience had hardened the ALI scheduling team.

Their main criterion was, as in everything else at the ALI, benefit to the learner. Whether the provider's chief executive was on vacation or not; whether the builders were going to be in or not; whether new and excellent procedures were being introduced or not; learners were there, probably in the midst of their only opportunity to get ahead in life. Seen from their point of view, a period of disruption in a provider is the ideal moment to test the robustness of its management and its commitment to learners' wellbeing.

The toolkit's second section dealt with 'preparing for inspection', complete with a checklist to help senior staff to be sure that they used the notice period productively; to be certain that everything possible was done to make the inspection a success.

The ALI inspector who was to lead the inspection then called the provider on the telephone, making the first personal contact and arranging to meet. A planning meeting was held, when the lead inspector would visit the provider and agree what needed to be done to collect secure evidence about the provider's performance: approximately how many observations; which areas of learning; what documentation; how many staff to be interviewed; how many employers or parents to be invited in to meet the inspectors; and so on.

A nominee from the provider's senior management would have been selected by the provider – according to advice on an appropriate choice issued by the ALI – and that person would have received a day's training in their task from the ALI. During that day, they would have had the chance to meet other providers' nominees, including some who had already been inspected and were able to give tips for success. The nominee would be part of the inspection team, an essential bridge between an external, independent view of a provider's work and that of its staff and managers.

There are two key elements of our quality improvement doctrine illustrated in all this. First, it is not the business of independent assessment to revel in the weakness of providers. If a provider works hard to improve itself during its three-month notice period and makes some significant changes, all well and good. How could that be anything other than beneficial to learners? Weak providers, in our experience, do not know how to improve. Given three months' or three years' notice, they would do no better, without guidance and stimulus to do things better. Second, 'no surprises'. Nothing should be done that the provider could not reasonably have expected and prepared for. Nothing should eventually be written in a published report about a provider that has not been clearly said at the time.

Candour. Openness. Transparency. Honesty. These things are fundamental to any debate that leads to quality improvement. If one of the parties to it is in a position of power, like a government inspectorate, then it must fall to that agency to create the circumstances in which they flourish. The provider cannot do it from a position of relative disadvantage. It follows that, by the time a properly organized external assessment of performance takes place, the confidence and trust needed to make observation of teaching and learning a helpful contribution should have been created. It will, of course, have demanded that managers go along with the programme of a body like the ALI, supporting its suggestions and encouraging staff, but our experience is that this is usually so, resting on the broad benefits gained from The Transformational Diamond.

The same kind of process needs to be gone through to prepare for the less tense business of internal or peer observation of teaching and learning. Those who are to be observed need to be reassured that those who will do the observing know their business. This is normally a 'given' with independent inspectors trained over many months to do the job, but by no means so within a single provider or a group whose members have agreed to help one another. Training observers is therefore an added task to be completed in these cases.

These are the things needed to make observation of teaching and learning productive:

- careful design of a scheme for routine use of observation as a means of quality improvement, intended to be carried out regularly and permanently;
- genuine consultation with staff, seeking to build a culture of continuous improvement;
- absolutely clear communication of the agreed scheme, both face to face by managers and in widely published form;
- clarity about any relationship between observations and staff performance review;
- painstaking training for both the observers and the observed;

- briefing for learners, so that they know what to expect during observed sessions;
- a plan for a round of observations, including analysis and presentation of the outcomes and allocation of resources and time to deal with shortcomings;
- a protocol for feedback, including timelines, appropriate environments and behaviours, the extent of confidentiality and record-keeping;
- agreement on a system of review or appeal, so that there is no reasonable expectation of unfairness.

This is no light undertaking. It will occupy a great deal of time among almost the whole staff of an organization. It is expensive of time and effort. If it is done badly, all that cost will have been wasted and, as our Case Study 4 illustrates, a single disastrous exchange can compromise the whole scheme. There will be high expectations of its accuracy among managers and the governing bodies or boards to which they present its outcome. If there is any laxity, any settled tendency to do other than give an honest view, to tell it like it is – and there is every human reason to be gentle with friends and colleagues – a scheme of observation will give false reassurance about the quality of the core of a learning organization's activities.

We have seen this happen with tragic consequences. A further education college had convinced itself and its board of the sustained excellence of its teaching and learning through using an observation scheme over a number of years. An independent inspection team was able to show convincingly that this was not so. The average grade awarded by college assessors was at least one grade point too high on our four-point scale. The loss of confidence in the chief executive among both his subordinate staff and his superintending board was catastrophic.

This is, however, no reason not to observe; no reason not to seek to know just how strong or weak a learning organization is in delivering its core business. It is a compelling reason not to enter into it lightly.

WHAT DOES GOOD LEARNING LOOK LIKE?

At the beginning of this chapter we commented on the distinction between teaching and learning. It could be said with a good deal of truth that the definition of good teaching is that it brings about vivid learning, in large amounts, in every learner present. Our point is that all this cannot be ascertained by looking at the teacher alone. And, of course, as we have also said, a great deal of adult learning goes on in the absence of a teacher. How are we to evaluate that?

The traditional stereotype of the inspector is of someone sitting at the back of a classroom, watching the teacher at the front and making notes. The kinds of things that would prompt a sentence or two are these:

- Did the teacher arrive promptly?
- Were latecomers noticed and remarked upon, encouraging punctuality next time?
- Was an accurate register kept of those present and absent and did it match the inspector's headcount?
- Did the teacher ensure that everyone in the lesson was visible, could hear what was said and was attending?
- Did the teacher introduce the lesson clearly, setting out what was to be done and what would be gained by the end?
- Was the teacher's material well organized, with a written lesson plan relevant to the syllabus and correctly pitched for the ability of the learners?
- Did the teacher regularly check that different members of the class understood what they were being taught, by asking searching, directed questions?
- Did the teacher use a variety of learning activities to ensure that everyone's interest was held, including such techniques as small-group discussion, quizzes, practical demonstrations and audio-visual aids?
- Did the teacher sum up succinctly the learning points from the lesson, often reinforcing them with well-chosen work to be done independently before the next meeting of the group?
- Did the lesson end promptly, allowing the class time to reach their next lesson?

■ Was homework or written coursework handed back promptly with helpful comments on each learner's work to help them do better next time?

These questions are valuable, but they refer most easily to formal teaching. There is an element of audit in them – was the teacher accurately marking the official register and was the state therefore getting value from the salary paid to the teacher? This reflects the regulatory aspect of traditional inspection, its concern with compliance and accountability for public resources. The inspector is directly evaluating the teacher's performance: organization, presentation, the ability to include and energize everyone present. Evidence of the learners' responses is, to some extent, second-hand. They are mostly seen from behind.

In the circumstances usual in most adult learning environments, even those where formal teaching takes place, these potential shortcomings can be alleviated. The observer does not have to sit at the empty desk at the back. The seating can usually be moved around to create a horseshoe around the teacher, or clustered in small groups. In the many practical sessions, the teacher usually moves about, guiding each individual learner. The 'howlers' we have seen – a small clique of friends chatting unobserved and unchecked behind a pillar, perhaps – are normally avoided. But by no means always! The simple things about organizing a space for learning and ensuring that what goes on in it is lively, engaging and available to everyone are sometimes overlooked, to the chagrin of the teacher when pointed out. Our comments about providing equality of opportunity to learn are at the nub of things, here. If familiarity can make us all blind to our surroundings, then shrewd observation can open our eyes again, particularly in that great mass of middling provision where teaching is adequate but uninspiring.

More useful for our purposes is an evaluation that puts learning first. We can ask whether learning is going on effectively and then what part teaching and a clutch of other contributions are playing. Let us consider work-based learning as an example. The learner is, first and foremost, an employee. There is a job of work to be done, with a wage attached to it. Learning and personal development are acknowledged as being important but it is likely that, at some time, there will be a rush of orders and everyone will come to the view that the apprentices should help fulfil it, the value in the experience of dealing with an emergency outweighing an interruption in attending day-release classes at the local college. There is a different conception of learning here, which does not necessarily rate formal teaching very highly among the various experiences available.

Work-based learning can be very rich. It includes daily mixing with older, more experienced people; an environment where real products and services are made and real customers show their pleasure or distaste in tangible ways; routine work on industry-standard equipment including, in examples we have seen, jet airliners which tomorrow will be taking passengers on their holidays; the availability of powerful incentives and disincentives – a wage rise or the sack; and availability of the resources to make learning really memorable. At Land Rover, for example, apprentices are sent away for a week or two each year in a group, to help a community in the developing world. They have built and equipped a school in Africa, and stayed in touch with its progress and its children. The learning experiences one could take from work-based learning might be these:

- technical expertise;
- familiarity with advanced technology;
- secure operational skill, refined through practice;
- effective teamwork;
- professional interaction with peers and superiors;
- creativity and adaptability;
- timekeeping, hard work and good professional habits of delivery to deadlines;
- consciousness of cost in relation to benefit;
- costing;
- sensitivity to the views of end-users.

And much else besides.

Work-based training, done well, will in other words deliver not only knowledge but also those 'soft skills' concerned with working productively with other people that are prized by businesses the world over. If a quality assessment process is to contribute materially to the improvement of all these things, observation must necessarily be developed in a broader sense than that needed in traditional inspection.

The people to be observed will be more various and, unlike the trained teacher who might be expected to be familiar with the kind of interpersonal dynamics found in observation, many of them will be completely unprepared for the process. They will include learners themselves, their supervisors, their managers and instructional staff at work as well, perhaps, as the teachers at the college which they attend for a day a week or so. The approach cannot be authoritarian. It cannot assume shared membership of an educational profession or vocation. It must include skilful questioning as well as watching. It must be done in a hundred and one different environments, including a good many with which the observer is bound to be unfamiliar and is the stranger. It must be fitted in round work. It must include an opportunity for the kind of helpful feedback that might be the only thing that the person concerned – who may very well never read the inspection report (after all, he or she is a car manufacturer, a chef, an accountant) – will ever take from the experience.

There are lessons in this which have general applicability, including to accurate observation of formal teaching and learning. They are that observation must be conducted with humility. The observer is seeking to know and understand, in order to help. Audit on behalf of a higher authority has to be diminished as an impression. Observation has to be done at the convenience of the observed, not the observer, even if that entails travelling to a workplace on the other side of the country or holding an interview during the night-shift at 3 am. Everything possible must be done to eliminate fear. Observation must reveal and celebrate what works for the learner, not what the textbooks mandate as good practice or, a term we abhor, 'best practice'. (Who is to say what works best for a particular learner?)

In this model, the quality assessor is the servant of learners and learning, the mirror reflecting and clarifying experience. The assessor is not the agent of a higher power, bringing the received wisdom against which what is seen can be compared.

MAKING OBSERVATION CREDIBLE

What has to be done to make this transaction work well?

First, the assessor's credibility must be established in the eyes of the observed. We mentioned earlier the importance of ensuring that external quality assessors, at least, had professional credibility. Only engineers should assess engineering, and so forth. Many professions are exclusive, using their own shorthand language, jargon, among initiates. We once committed what was seen as an appalling gaffe by suggesting that the armed services' use of initials and numbers to define practically everything might hinder the acclimatization of new recruits to the military life. We were told in no uncertain terms that military usage had been developed to reduce the chances of orders being misunderstood in the chaos of combat. The sooner recruits learned this new 'language', the safer they were likely to be on their first operational encounter. That may well be true. Even if one retains a touch of scepticism, it makes no sense to risk the mirror held up to the learning experience by observation being distorted by a presumption of 'otherness' from the outset. We need independence to observe accurately, but we also need empathy.

We cannot over-egg this point. In our country, with its wealth of inspection experience from which to draw lessons, there remain voices arguing that inspection is itself a profession. 'Once trained as an inspector, you can inspect anything' is the claim. Our experience strongly suggests otherwise. We have seen, several times repeated in different countries, initial enthusiasm to set up a government inspectorate wrecked by the appointment of a group of ill-starred junior civil servants to do the job. In many countries, public service is regarded as second best to the private sector; they were handicapped simply by working for their government. Their inexperience, their lack of professional achievement, their terms of employment determining hours of work different from those of the organizations they were supposed to visit and improve – all these things amounted to a lack of credibility which doomed the whole enterprise from the start.

Whether internal, peer or independent, observations should be conducted by respected senior practitioners from the same professional background as the people being observed. Nothing else will give the lessons a fair chance of sticking. Anything else offers too many hostages to fortune, too many opportunities for easy dismissal of unpalatable suggestions for change. If it is possible to introduce an element of *vox populi*, selection by peer acknowledgement or acclaim for internal or peer observation schemes, so much the better.

Acceptability is also secured by thorough training. Once the right people have been chosen, they need to be prepared for a new task. It took at least six months to train an ALI inspector, on and off the job. Training for the narrower role of observation will not take so long, but a half-day workshop will not suffice.

The consistency of observation is helped greatly by use of a standard form to note down what was seen and said, and first impressions derived from them. We suggest a simple layout in Figure 4.2, which has already been completed to illustrate its use.

Given the variety of learning experiences we suggest need to be observed in TVET, it is hard to generalize about how long each one should take. However, it is unlikely that any reliable information can be collected in less than 30–45 minutes, bearing in mind that we should be looking for some evidence of predetermined organization, of pattern, even in the most informal learning. And the person being observed needs some assurance that enough time has been spent to gather a fair sample of the learning experience as well.

What do we mean by pattern? We share a background in the visual arts and design. In our early days as inspectors we were struck by the fact that we often saw college classes where work of very high quality was being produced and where the students, when questioned, spoke articulately and with passion about what they were doing and what they were learning. Yet there seemed to be little or no teaching going on. Typically the teacher would go from student to student, enquiring whether they were getting on all right and leaving them with an encouraging word if they answered 'yes', or talking about possibilities and options for exploration with those who were stuck. What gave this apparently shapeless set of exchanges a strong pattern was that the students were working independently to create a personal solution to a project brief set by the teacher. Patterning was provided by the logical structure and clear set of demands of the brief and its relationship to an overall scheme of work; the quality of the introductory teaching, exploring both ideas and new skills; the formative assessments made as the work went forward; and the summative group critique at the end, in which lessons were drawn from everyone's triumphs and disasters in a positive way, for the benefit of the whole group.

Provider:	City College	Sheet no: 3
Inspector's name: A N Other		Date: 4/10/07
Area of learning: Engineering		Qualification aim: Apprenticeship/NVQ3
Subject/programme Mechanical Engineering		
Description of context & mode of learning: (eg Classroom – part-time, distance learning, on-the-job, simulated work etc) Theory in training centre classroom		Location: College
No. of learners present: 14	No. on register/ expected: 17	Length of observation (minutes): 60
Consider Common Inspection Framework key questions on: • Learners' achievements and progress • Effectiveness of teaching and learning • Appropriateness of resources • Assessment practices • Appropriateness of programme • Support for learners • Effectiveness of leadership and management in raising achievement and supporting all learners • Effectiveness of assuring the quality of teaching, training and learning • Effectiveness of the promotion of equality of opportunity.		

Strengths: Clear initial summary of session aims
Good use of whiteboards and display materials
Range of activities to stimulate discussion and interest
Good summary and conclusion to session by tutor

Weaknesses: 4 late arrivals disrupted first 10 mins
Participation by learners was patchy and some were inattentive throughout
Little use of questioning to establish learning
Tutor failed to involve all class members in activities

Other information needed:
Reinforce theory through writing or referral to handouts

Overall evaluation of learning session:
The first half of the session failed to grab the attention of all the learners. The trainer worked hard, using whiteboard and visual aids, to generate discussion but some of the group were lethargic and unresponsive. (Session was immediately after lunch on a very hot day and the room temperature was high.) The second activity was better received but participation was still incomplete. Several of the pairs tasked with working together to solve a problem failed to work on the task. However, the tutor made good use of the available feedback from this exercise to encourage learners to work more effectively on the next piece of work.

Note any examples of good or poor practice:

Grade:	4	1 – excellent, 2 – good, 3 – satisfactory, 4 – inadequate

Figure 4.2   An observation form

Looked at with professional understanding and an emphasis on the value of the learning rather than the appearance of the teaching, such sessions were often judged very favourably.

It is helpful to disrupt the session as little as possible. Anything approaching interference or encroachment on the 'teaching' role, whatever that may be in a particular case, is almost certainly counterproductive. It certainly precludes objective judgement about the true interaction between that teacher and that learner or learners. While it may be an almost agonizing temptation to intervene when a young teacher is being dismantled by a clamorous class, it is better to withdraw quietly, perhaps coming back to observe the same person with a different group.

GIVING THE MESSAGES

The real purpose of observation, with guidance for improvement firmly in mind, is feedback. There is no real point in observation unless a decent opportunity is created for feedback, beyond the collection of a small piece of data which will contribute to an overall judgement on the quality of teaching and learning in that provider. That may satisfy external quality assessors and the provider's senior managers, but it is of scant help in raising capability in the organization's main task. The frustration of the teacher, observed but not informed, can readily be imagined.

It is, however, often difficult to arrange enough time and the right circumstances for feedback, particularly during an external evaluation when the pressure is on to collect and assimilate a vast quantity of information in a few days. This is what should be done, probably in only 5 or 10 minutes:

- Arrange a time and place for feedback either in advance or at the end of an observation.
- Find somewhere private and quiet, where it is possible to concentrate on ensuring that the teacher gets the right message.
- Arrange the seating to give a relaxed atmosphere, ideally with chairs at right-angles to one another, at a table or freestanding.

- Take care that the circumstances are not uncomfortably intimate; for example, that people of opposite sexes are not sitting knee-to-knee in easy chairs.
- Be courteous; thank the teacher for their time and cooperation.
- Plan what you are going to say in advance and make brief notes you can refer to easily.
- Be quiet and calm: never heated, over-assertive or argumentative.
- Always begin with the strengths of what you have seen, going on to weaknesses and areas for improvement when a positive discussion has been firmly established.
- If you have hard messages to give, be straight and clear, but not brutal.
- Do not allow the conversation to slip into comment about what the teacher *is*, rather than what you have seen them *do*; this is a discussion about practice on a single occasion, not personality.
- Give suggestions about ways to develop or improve and, if you are observing as part of an internal scheme, make sure that you arrange the necessary support.
- Be firm about ending the feedback on the terms you planned, with a summary emphasizing strengths on which to build for the future.

This is known irreverently by inspectors as a 'good news sandwich'. The filling of criticism is always placed between two slices of praise bread. The intention is far from cynical. It is to achieve the greatest possible chance that teachers will regard observation as a welcome contribution to their own professional development, helping them to do a hard job beautifully. Refer again and again to benefit to learners, the people that the teacher almost certainly cares most about, and even difficult changes are usually taken on board. While this kind of observation is not primarily a form of teacher training, but rather the collection of evidence on which the organization is to be judged, it should be useful and memorable for the teacher.

To end this chapter, let us deal with three thorny topics. These are grading of observations, confidentiality and the use of observation for performance management.

The arguments for and against grading individual observations are much the same as those related to organizations. Grades summarize, are unmistakable, and can be aggregated to show trends or provide comparisons with benchmarks. They turn a set of individual quality interventions into guidance for the improvement of the whole organization. Those are such valuable advantages that, in our view, they are too good to miss.

However, there is a valid debate about whether the grade should be given to the teacher at the feedback. The points in favour of doing so are strong: that the whole process is designed to be transparent, carefully building trust. The arguments against are pragmatic: a grade given by an observer may well be provisional, subject to moderation by someone else to assure consistency of judgement across the whole organization; it can be annoyingly disruptive and run counter to the emphasis on observed performance rather than personal virtue, if someone leaves a feedback boasting loudly to colleagues 'I am a grade 1 teacher!' We hesitate to advise, because the answer to this dilemma is likely to depend on the maturity and level of trust that exist within each organization. However, as far as independent, external observations are concerned, it is probably best to stick to the conservative view. If in doubt, do not share observation grades, but explain very clearly why you are not doing so.

Second, we come to confidentiality. We do not believe that external or peer observers should share their views about an individual teacher with managers. We say that unequivocally. Our conviction springs from the fact that one or two observations are a wholly insufficient basis for a judgement which, if passed to managers, might blight an individual's future career. It is the job of managers to monitor the performance of staff, not that of visitors, however expert or well intentioned. We have often been asked by senior managers which teachers were awarded low grades. We never tell them, whatever blandishments or pressures are brought to bear. But we do point out that good managers know their staff.

However, the case may well be altered where observations are carried out by managers, specifically for the purpose of performance management. There, feedback, or at least its salient points, should be specifically understood as open to others and should be recorded and agreed by both parties just like any other appraisal which may influence bonus payments, promotion or job security. We would expect that several observations would be made before any conclusion was reached. There is nothing wrong with observation as part of performance management. Indeed, it is normal in our country nowadays. But it is as much part of the human resources structure of an organization as of its quality improvement procedures. Its format and safeguards should reflect that.

Inevitably, in this chapter we have concentrated a good deal on methods. We want to end it where we started. Good teaching – let us not mince words – *great* teaching – is inspirational and transformational. Only in the past few hundred years of human history has it been an organized, formal business, mainly concentrated in state institutions set up for the purpose. Before that, learning was fostered within families and clan groups, where life-skills and job-skills intermingled and were passed on side by side. This is sometimes derided as 'Sitting by Nelly'; the picture conjured up supposed to be of a youngster sitting next to an elderly female relative, learning by watching and copying.

However, there is scant evidence that human genius was stunted by this process. The record suggests otherwise. There are many more of us now, family bonds are often weaker and families more dispersed. The pace of change is much higher, the body of knowledge more extensive. That is the rationale for the existence of schools, colleges and universities. But let us emphasize that, even in the most developed countries and economies, most learning goes on in the family, at work, or with friends and neighbours in the community. List, if we do not convince you, the number of people you know who are doing the job for which their studies directly prepared them; the people you know whose real flair and talent are shown in what they do in their spare time, rather than the way they earn their living.

Observation schemes and observers of learning should never lose sight of that. Great teaching and learning can be unexpected, unconventional. More of it is informal than formal. It can be helped along by the sympathetic observer who wants to add to the merits of what is already there, but it is shrivelled up by the attentions of the dusty pedant.

Case Study 4

Feedback: what can go wrong, will go wrong

In a training workshop which included delegates from many countries, experienced inspectors advised on how to give feedback to teachers whose lessons had just been observed. They included demonstrations. An inspector played the part of a very experienced teacher who felt his professional integrity to be threatened by observation of one of his lessons. He complained loudly that he was always under pressure through lack of time. Both the observation and the feedback added to that pressure, he said.

A woman inspector carefully arranged chairs so that she was able to give feedback in a relaxed atmosphere, but without getting too close to the 'teacher'. She spoke to him quietly and calmly, acknowledging his concerns and praising his considerable strengths. She also clearly identified weaknesses in his approach to teaching and classroom management, suggesting carefully that these probably contributed to the pressure on his time. She ended by proposing and agreeing with him a clear set of changes to be made and the support he would be given to see them through.

The delegates were convinced that what they had been shown would work well in their own countries. They discussed the need to plan and control the discussion carefully and to use position, tone of voice, and language in an effort to ensure that points were understood and accepted. They then split into groups to try the techniques for themselves.

A young male manager from a culture in which men usually were dominant acted as the 'inspector', feeding back to a middle-aged woman. He prepared very briefly what he wanted to say and the shape he intended for the interview. Both 'inspector' and 'teacher' remained standing. The 'inspector' had his notes on a clipboard, which he held in one hand while poking a pen at the 'teacher' with the other to emphasize his points.

He began by asking whether she would like to hear his assessment of her strengths or weaknesses first. She meekly asked for the latter. He began to tell her very assertively about her faults in approach and teaching method. The 'teacher' at first listened quietly and then began to challenge what she was being told with increasing confidence. The 'inspector' started to argue and then was silenced. From his initial position, standing less than a metre from the 'teacher', he backed away until blocked, perched uncomfortably on the corner of a table. He drew the clipboard in close to his chest, like a shield, and pointed the pen towards himself, his right hand twisted awkwardly in order to do so. From a bold, chest-out, posture, he hunched and narrowed his shoulders under the 'teacher's' onslaught.

The delegates were amused and delighted that someone apparently so over-confident had been routed by a smaller, more junior woman. The 'inspector' had failed to feed back any of the positive points and most of the issues that needed improvement from the observation he had made. His authority was wholly lost. It would have been difficult or even impossible to make a new start with the interview.

Had a genuine exchange like this taken place between a teacher and a manager in the same organization as part of a performance management procedure, both the relationship and the scheme would have been badly undermined. The exchange illustrated all too well the dangers of ill-planned observation of a teacher at work, by someone inadequately trained either to analyse accurately what he had seen or to give feedback to the teacher in a controlled and constructive way. He began by attempting to exert power, rather than give support. He ended as a victim.

Note

1   Moser, C (1999) *A Fresh Start*, TSO, London

5

Using self-assessment

Most mature quality assessment and improvement schemes now include self-assessment. In England, compulsory self-assessment for learning providers spending public money began with further education colleges in 1994. It was extended to work-based learning in 1998 and to the rest of adult TVET in 2001. The government funding agencies require production of a self-assessment report every year, using as a basis the same framework as the inspectorate. Mature, certainly, but the reliability of self-assessment is less sure. Many providers are too kind in making judgements about themselves for the results to be of much use in driving them on to outstanding performance in the globalized world.

The last comprehensive comparison between self-assessment grades and inspection grades was published by the ALI at the end of 2004.[1] Providers used the same grading scale for self-assessment as did ALI inspectors. Providers graded themselves 93 per cent satisfactory or better in delivering occupational training, compared with 66 per cent according to the independent inspectors. For their own leadership and management, providers assessed themselves as 90 per cent satisfactory or better, compared with 65 per cent awarded by the inspectors. In the first case, providers' self-assessment judgements were more favourable than that of the independent inspectors by 27 percentage points and, in the second, by 25 percentage points. There was very little difference in the size of the gap between providers that had been producing self-assessments for a decade and those that were new to it.

We should not be surprised. The ALI commented at the time, 'In a competitive contracting environment, providers often shy away from admitting to faults and move on to exaggerating their strengths.' It takes real bravery to tell the people who authorize your finance that your work is poor, before they come and find out for themselves. Most people hope against hope that they can hide their problems away. While there are some providers that genuinely have no idea how bad a service they offer, most just give themselves the benefit of any doubt.

It is not hard to imagine how that process of rounding off every uncomfortable sharp edge takes place. Observing your friends and colleagues at work and telling them they are not good enough is likely to make big waves. The people who really know where the problems are tend to be those in closest contact with learners, the people near the bottom of the hierarchy. Telling your boss that things are not good is like writing a suicide note in some organizations. As Ron Heifetz and Marty Linsky of Harvard University put it:

> Every day brings you opportunities to raise important questions, speak to higher values and surface unresolved conflicts. Every day you have the chance to make a difference in the lives of people around you. And every day you must decide whether to put your contribution out there or keep it to yourself to avoid upsetting anyone, and get through another day. You are right to be cautious.... You risk people's ire and make yourself vulnerable.[2]

Organizations where challenge and questioning from the bottom of the heap are accepted, or even welcomed, are all too rare in our experience. Shooting the messenger rather than reading the message is one of the bad habits of the corporate world, whether the organization is a public sector college or a blue-chip private enterprise. Those that take note of the bad news as well as the good, and do something about it, are sometimes, but not always, today's global winners, but we have no doubt that a robust, self-critical culture will be one of the marks of tomorrow's even more pressured top dogs. Authoritarian cultures rely on one person's creativity, while self-critical organizations benefit from everybody's. That includes their customers.

So self-assessment is worth doing, even if we have to take some of the results with a pinch of salt. We have to have faith in it as a direction of travel, accepting Ronald Reagan's already-quoted scepticism in 'Trust, but verify' – and not allowing ourselves to slip into Lenin's cynicism: 'Trust is good but control is better.'

TWINS

Self-assessment and independent assessment are necessary bedfellows, the first informing and enriching the second, and the second keeping the first honest. That seems to us a realistic and effective settlement as organizations work towards global competitiveness, with but one proviso. The procedures involved have to be kept simple and efficient, avoiding the creation of an industry, scrutiny heaped on scrutiny, to the infuriation of everyone concerned.

Let us give you an example of what to avoid. In England, further education colleges launched into regular inspection, underpinned by regular self-assessment. Their uncertainties about self-assessment prompted them to get professional advice. Still not feeling secure, they often commissioned a 'pre-inspection inspection' in an effort to bridge the gap between self-assessment results and those that might come out of an independent assessment. A host of consultancies geared up to do the job. Then the funding body decided that it needed more regular reassurance, so it set up a quality monitoring framework of its own, based on a 'balanced scorecard' of numerical indicators which may or may not have been a useful contribution to self-assessment and inspection. Tiring of the expense and bureaucracy involved in all this, the government moved in to make the independent inspection process weaker, less frequent, in the apparently reasonable name of 'proportionality to risk', so finally destroying the original balance between self-assessment and independent verification. To avoid slithering down this slippery slope, you need a firm grip on the basic principles involved. If you are a provider, you have to take responsibility yourself for keeping a sense of proportion, for not getting panicked.

In this chapter, the last dealing with the Assessment facet of The Transformational Diamond, we urge you never to forget the old acronym KISS: 'Keep it simple, stupid!' Self-assessment should be right for you, right for the scale and nature of your organization, providing accountability to others so far as the essentials are concerned but no more.

All assessment, including self-assessment if it is well conceived and well conducted, offers three things: regulation, accountability and improvement (Figure 5.1).

Accountability

AIR

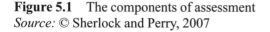

Regulation ———— Improvement

Figure 5.1   The components of assessment
Source: © Sherlock and Perry, 2007

LOVING SELF-ASSESSMENT

The one component that may not appear to sit easily with self-assessment is regulation. Regulation is about obeying the rules and being able to demonstrate that you obey the rules. Certainly, it is often, or even usually, associated with something done to operational organizations by someone with official powers. But even a quick look beneath the surface reveals something else. Take, for example, the production and audit of financial accounts, a process at its most stringent, probably, in the public sector worldwide where the idea of a higher duty to taxpaying fellow citizens is firmly rooted in the psyche of management. Accounts are produced by organizations themselves. The 'accounting officer' in British public bodies, the person responsible for any and all financial indiscretion, is the chief executive. It is the chief executive who signs the accounts and the 'statement on internal control', certifying that there have been no lapses. The auditors, the apparent regulators, just give 'reasonable assurance that' (the accounts signed in blood by the chief executive) 'are free from material misstatement whether caused by fraud or error'.

That is an additional comfort to the public or to private shareholders, and a very important one, but the preparation of the accounts and the acceptance of responsibility for them are firmly internal matters. They are a matter of self-assessment, checked on a sample basis by an independent body. Publication of the audited accounts is probably the discipline that bites hardest. If a learning provider's self-assessment is treated with the seriousness applied to the annual accounts, there is no reason why it should not be seen as fulfilling part of its regulatory needs. And if it were published, woe betide the provider caught out in a lie!

Accountability is easier. Accountability is a matter of being open, being responsible, to stakeholders. For any organization taking public money, it is fair to say that those stakeholders include not only the owners (shareholders or government), but also learners, their families and their employers, and the staff. Once again, publication of an open and honest self-assessment would do the job. Social responsibility, among both private sector and public or charitable bodies, is a feature of the globalized world, as we suggested in Chapter 1.

And finally, improvement. Just being open and accountable is important, but self-assessment is expensive. It occupies a great deal of the time of everyone in an organization. It would seem wasteful not to use it as a means for summing up what has been achieved and what has not and setting some new, higher, goals for the coming year.

What might the features of self-assessment fulfilling all these functions be?

- It should be regular and reasonably frequent.
- It should be based on similar evidence to that used by independent quality assessors.
- It should focus on what is of importance in providing benefit for learners.
- It should follow the same framework as is used by external quality assessors.
- It should be candid and self-critical.
- It should draw systematically on the views of the main stakeholders and involve all those inside the organization.
- It should be summed up in a succinct report, which refers to the evidence for judgements and states where it can be found.
- It should use the same numerical grades, summarizing judgements about the same areas of activity, as external quality assessors.

■ It should show trends over time.

■ It should set clearly defined targets for the work to be done to build on strengths and remedy weaknesses.

■ The self-assessment report should be published, at least in summary.

The reason we suggest that self-assessment should be strongly guided by the requirements of external quality assessors is entirely pragmatic and has nothing to do with authority. It is to avoid duplicating effort and wasting time.

We have sometimes been puzzled why it is that learning providers so often become desperately anxious about self-assessment. We see it as commonsense, an almost automatic by-product of good management. Other than the features we propose above, we have never specified the form of self-assessment, in the hope that each provider would develop something suited to its own culture and needs. Nevertheless, the desire to follow a pattern is often strong even when, as is generally the case, imposed patterns are over-engineered because they attempt to deal with even the biggest, most complex organization.

Over-complexity in self-assessment makes the process, and the report summarizing it, a burden. If it becomes a burden, organizations quickly lose the will to do it wholeheartedly and the results will not justify however little effort is made. Discontent sets in and an important means to achieve global competitiveness is lost. Managers have an important job to do, finding a shape and scale for self-assessment that keeps it fresh, keeps it interesting and keeps it possible as part of the routine of the organization. As we hint in Figure 5.1, self-assessment should bring in fresh AIR, not fog.

Let us give you an example of largely unnecessary anxiety. Nicky Perry once led the external quality assessment of an organization which acted as an employment agency for ballet dancers and kept them in training while they waited for work. It saw itself as artistic, a little anarchic and hostile to what it regarded as the tedious routines of self-assessment. The chief executive gave up the ghost from the start, inviting Perry to award the organization a poor grade for its quality assurance.

She took the challenge well, offering to point out the self-critical routines already in daily use. There was the dancing master, supervising the work of the teacher taking dancers through their daily exercises at the barré. There were the rough notes, recording the fitness and readiness for work of each dancer. There was the weekly staff meeting, where every dancer was discussed; their progress, their injuries and their suitability for the jobs coming in. It was informal, intuitive, deeply rooted in the collective experience and professional discipline of staff who were themselves strictly trained in classical dance. As Perry pointed out, all that was necessary was a little more formality in record-keeping to ensure that the system was proof against changes of key staff and capable of teasing out and analysing lessons for development over time.

At the other end of the spectrum, we have seen apprentices in aero engine and airframe maintenance, where the routines and records already required by the air safety authorities provided more than enough raw material for regulation and accountability. Continuous improvement was necessarily a cautious business, but one for which all the data on which to base it were readily available. Self-assessment was culturally natural – in other words, as natural as breathing. For that reason, organizations like Rolls-Royce, Marshall Aerospace and Monarch Airlines, all British-based companies whose training we have independently assessed on several occasions, thrive on the process and are confirmed by it as being world-class.

Good self-assessment is encouraged from the top. It has to be, because it demands the existence of corporate values that nourish open and honest self-criticism. If the chief executive cannot bear hearing reservations expressed about his or her behaviours and effectiveness, and gives everyone to understand that openness is unwelcome, then the process will be crippled from the start. Sometimes the messages that float to the top will seem like rough justice or plain wrong. 'We never see you' may be true and will probably be met with the excuse that dealing with external stakeholders, the board, the long-term future of the organization, wipes out time for walking the job. From the point of view of learners – the most important arbiters of what is or is not appropriate in our Framework – it matters profoundly that the boss is visible, accessible, knows what is really going on. Sitting in an office hatching plans is not good management. Learners will not be slow to tell you so and they will be right.

Fostering openness is not about creating a clutch of representative committees. It is about ensuring that the people who matter most in this business, the learners, feel that their judgement about the service they get matters and will be quickly heard at the level where decisions are made and change is authorized. That may require a formal structure in a large organization. However, in a smaller unit, it may well suffice if everyone from the chief executive down works in an open environment, in which people are encouraged to talk to one another and share information when they need to, rather than go for the paraphernalia of formal meetings. They should be reserved for the purpose for which they were intended: making corporate decisions.

GETTING IT DONE

Let us suppose then that our public or private organization is culturally ready for self-assessment. People talk to one another. There is trust, but also active management which delivers change when it is found to be necessary. People who say something that is true and express it in a civilized way are not scapegoated, even if their message is upsetting. How, then, do we go about self-assessment?

Our experience is that leadership of self-assessment, as well as representation of the provider's point of view during independent assessment, is best done by someone near the top but not at the top. That person should be trusted by the chief executive and by more junior staff. They should have easy access to all the records revealing corporate performance in learning. In larger organizations this person might well be a quality director or quality manager, sometimes concerned with the products or services the organization sells as well as the training it offers. Almost all UK colleges have a dedicated quality manager, a facility that has evolved over time under the goad of routine external quality assessment. In very small learning organizations there may only be one owner-manager, in which case the job falls to that person.

The argument against having the chief executive do the job is that there will be prompts for change coming from any good self-assessment and the boss's job will be to prioritize them and drive them through. It works best if prescription and action are separate.

English inspectorates call the leader of self-assessment, who is usually also the organization's representative on an external assessment team, 'the provider's nominee'. It is not a good term. It implies something altogether too passive, at least as far as self-assessment is concerned. However, it does imply that in one person, the whole of an organization's effort in delivering learning quality is gathered together. They represent everyone, rather than necessarily controlling everyone.

In self-assessment, the 'nominee' usually brings a small team together to do the work. They need to be representative of all the important facets of the organization and they should be enthusiasts. There is a lot of work to be done, a lot of communication to pitch just right, and probably some challenging advocacy to push through.

Just like in external assessment, the task starts with collection of evidence. The effort made to ensure that the evidence is true, beyond reasonable challenge, is critically important. It will need to be 'triangulated' to guarantee that it is not just gossip, hearsay or a rogue statistic, out of tune with every other indicator. The great opportunity inherent in self-assessment is to ensure that the evidence is richer, more comprehensive than anything a team from outside the organization could ever amass in a week's inspection. This same evidence will be presented to the independent quality assessors. Here is the chance to find out what needs to be done and do it before it is imposed from outside. Collecting powerful evidence, verifying it, understanding what it means and responding appropriately are the real tests of an organization's maturity and its commitment to be outstanding.

Here are some of the types of evidence that will throw up answers to the questions in the Quality Assessment Framework:

- records from observations of teaching and learning;
- data on learners' achievements, tracked over three or more years to reveal trends;
- data on early leavers;
- data on learners' outcomes and progression to higher awards, better jobs or other successes;
- comparisons of learners' success in different areas or with different teachers;

- comparisons of the performance of learners of different genders, ethnic backgrounds, ages, prior educational achievements, or disabilities;
- feedback from learners, both analytical and qualitative;
- feedback from stakeholders;
- feedback from staff of all kinds;
- performance against targets set by the organization for itself following previous self-assessments or independent assessments;
- performance against benchmarks provided by similar providers or national and international surveys conducted by inspectorates, funding agencies, international agencies like the OECD or academic research;
- comparison with policy guidelines issued by governments and others;
- 'bottom line' data such as increased profitability through training or higher staff retention;
- efficiency data including usage of accommodation, equipment and staffing.

The list could obviously grow and grow. The trick in managing self-assessment well is to decide what the organization really has to know to raise its performance continuously, rather than what it might just be interesting to know (KISS). The information we have listed above should be collected routinely as a matter of performance management. It is the stuff of normal quality assurance. If it is collected routinely, then self-assessment consists of drawing it together every year or so, analysing it coolly and recommending what more has to be achieved to raise the organization's game overall.

Not all this information will be equally reliable. Handing out 'happy sheets' at the end of lessons, lectures or workshops is pretty much routine. They prompt an instant response to the qualities of the learning experience. It is a worthy enterprise, but not one that is usually suited to numerical tracking of, say, an individual trainer's performance over time, nor does it encourage deep reflection on what has been learnt. Similarly, learner satisfaction surveys are a commonplace in our country and a lot of self-congratulation follows when they bring good news. The trouble is that they almost always do, even when they are professionally designed and carried out with very large numbers of people.

The truth is that learners, and especially young learners, usually like and admire their teachers and have very few similar experiences on which to base a reliable comparison. Extreme discontent comes to the surface all right, but it is very rare. What can we do differently, having been told that 90 per cent of learners are satisfied or very satisfied with the service they get?

Better tends to be the information drawn from small focus groups, expertly conducted to explore a particular issue, or small surveys where the extreme responses are not obscured by the sheer volume in the middle ground. If you really want to know something from customers and stakeholders, it pays to define precisely what you want from them before you start. The test is 'what will this information guide us to *do*?'

DATA, DATA, DATA

There are notes of warning to be sounded in regard to data collection. Our experience in working with the armed services provides some useful pointers. At an infantry training depot in the north of England, we spoke with an officer who had for several years been carrying out exit interviews with young people who were leaving the Army before even completing their initial training. We were delighted to hear this, believing that he would have information that could help shape the means of reducing early drop-out, cutting back the waste of money and effort associated with an aborted recruitment and the distress of a young person with a 'failure' to their name. Our hopes were dashed on finding he had kept no record of all these interviews. He had not been asked to do so. He believed nobody would be interested in the results, even if he had taken the initiative to do so on his own.

People only strive to find out new things and to make recommendations for change if curiosity is specifically encouraged and they work in a data-rich environment.

Here is another military example from several years ago. Training establishments all over our country made detailed records of the number of recruits they received, some personal information about them – for example their gender, age, race and nationality – and what happened to them in training. As a disciplined force, they did as they were asked and passed this information to a national statistics unit. Very seldom did any information come back down the line. Very few of the officers we met expected it to. Neither did many of them analyse the statistics they collected before they sent them off to who-knows-where. The result was that they did most of the work to create a data-rich management environment, but received none of the benefits. They did not know, on anything better than a basis of anecdote, whether, for example, recruits from Samoa were more likely to be bullied or be bullies than those from Scotland, or whether more young women dropped out of training early than young men. Neither did the national data agency produce and disseminate composite information for all similar establishments, allowing commanding officers to look out for significant variations at their own.

These examples are clear-cut, but they are not unusual in our experience. Collecting information is a routine corporate activity in both the public and private sectors. It is expensive to do. Analysing it and interrogating it – making it into useful management information to guide decisions for action – is less common. The lesson is: do not collect data without knowing how they are to be used.

The issue of honesty in self-assessment we have already mentioned and it is, perhaps, too obvious to labour much further. However, it arises, usually unwittingly, whenever targets for improvement are set. Most targets, if sustained for some years, are capable of distorting performance and outcomes. People 'jump for the jellybeans' whether they are the right ones or not.

A dramatic national example in England was the use of a provider achievement measure for National Vocational Qualifications of 'NVQs per 100 leavers'. Because the qualification was competency based – you could do what was required or you could not; no half measures – it was thought logical by the funding bodies only to pay providers by results, when each learner had achieved the NVQ. The outcome was all too easily foreseeable, with the benefit of hindsight. Providers sometimes became assessment bucket-shops, diminishing the amount of training to a bare minimum to achieve the NVQ and cheating to amass NVQ 'successes' before learners had much by way of discernible skill. The more NVQs awarded the more profitable the provider, and the more quickly they were achieved the better the cash flow. Provider achievement measures of '150

NVQs per 100 leavers' were commonplace, rendering completely useless a performance benchmark intended to yield percentages. The corrective consisted of tougher supervision of assessment by the awarding bodies; dumping the 'NVQs per 100 leavers' measure; and introducing staged payments to providers matched to the activities that needed reinforcement. Payments were, for example, made to reward thoroughly conducted induction and at other points in The Learner's Journey, gradually contributing to restoring the integrity and reputation of the NVQ and building back the incentive to do new things.

There are many similar examples. If things can go wrong they will go wrong, and they always can go wrong. If the pressure applied to providers or to groups of staff in a learning organization is unfair or excessive, look out for falsified good results. It is a duty of managers not to offer excessive temptation and to select targets that will genuinely bring benefit to learners if they are met. The greater the anxiety among those managers, and in the competitive global market the managers of the system keen to get quick results can include everybody up to government ministers, the more likely they are to connive in hunting for quick wins, however illusory the gain will eventually turn out to be.

SELF-ASSESSING WHAT?

Finding a suitable unit for self-assessment is important in developing manageability. Should it be by department or faculty or subsidiary company or whole organization? The report will need to cover the whole organization and it is usually at the corporate level that data and quality management lie. The temptation to go for a big, all-embracing scheme is likely to be strong. However, there are virtues in breaking the whole thing up into bite-sized chunks in all but the smallest organizations. It is easier to truly involve everyone that way. They care and know most about their own tasks and their own learners. Self-assessment in a fairly small team can be an intimate and rewarding affair. Everyone knows each other well enough to feel secure. The challenge is, of course, to get some objectivity and push-back into the debate, so that it moves performance towards the leading edge.

That can be done by having a central team for the whole organization, whose members join small-unit staff to introduce a wider perspective and the key question for all self-assessment debates: 'So what?' Most people can contentedly deal with strengths and weaknesses in their own and their immediate colleagues' practice, provided that the tone of the discussion is hygienically theoretical. They will probably need bringing down to earth every now and then by a challenge that demands consideration of relevance and action. So what?

Small-team self-assessment can also throw up a wealth of comparative information, and the questions that go with it. 'Why is this staff group so much more successful in achieving good learner outcomes than that one, when learners' previous attainments look similar and the group uses much the same resources to develop them when they are here?' The responses can be kept honest by a central quality self-assessment team or by groups auditing each other. The value to be had from assessing parts of an organization, rather than all of it at once, is the creation of the classic quality assurance environment; one where it is possible to compare and contrast the performance of similar entities.

One of the benefits that might flow from breaking down self-assessment group by group is the option of staggering the process. In other words, if a complete self-assessment, fit for interrogation by independent quality assessors, has to be conducted every four years, why not take a quarter of the organization each year? That 'quarter' might be a representative sample of the whole organization; it might be a cluster of similar activities; it might be the areas of poor performance. There are advantages and disadvantages in each one. Provided that the quarters can sensibly and easily be brought together every four years to give a comprehensive, fair and reasonably current account of the whole organization, the choice will be determined by what seems right for the company.

Keep it simple. Keep it interesting. Keep it fresh. Keep moving the organization forward. Keep an end in mind.

A SELF-CRITICAL CULTURE

We probably need a further word about organizational culture. It is a distressingly vague idea, hard to grasp, hard to change in any planned way. And yet, as everyone who works with others knows, it is the difference between going off every morning with a spring in your step, eagerly looking forward to getting on with the job, and employment as drudgery. If you like the people you work with and for; if you feel valued and respected; if you feel that your contribution really counts; if you feel that what the organization does is worthwhile; if you feel decently paid; if you could happily recommend working at your company or buying its products to friends; then the culture is probably healthy.

Many polling organizations conduct surveys, covering aspects of staff opinion about their employers. They should figure prominently in every sound self-assessment. The reason is that staff satisfaction is the single most reliable predictor of customer satisfaction.

No employer can control every transaction between staff and customers. That is true especially in larger organizations with remote sites. However smart an organization is in its financial management, its policies and procedures, however excellent its product, it will drive away customers if its frontline staff are surly and unhelpful. If there is a violent dissonance between the advertised service and the one that customers actually experience, their disappointment and annoyance will be all the greater. If managers can do one thing to assure corporate success, it is to love their staff, to do everything possible to make them feel good.

That may seem obvious. However, it is not simply a matter of paying them more than anyone else, as all the long-established management research shows. This is because money is not a motivator but simply something that we come to expect and regard as our due just a few months after we have been given a raise. Enriching corporate cultures, much the same as national cultures, depends on the big things: justice, honesty, transparency, openness to reasonable criticism and challenge, fairness, conscientiousness. Those are the things that make self-assessment possible and rewarding. Those are the things that, fundamentally, delight staff and delight the customers whom they serve.

A footnote. According to the polling company MORI, the norm for staff satisfaction in public sector organizations – in the UK at least – is markedly lower than for the private sector. There is an apparent paradox there which we have not got to the bottom of. However, our experience is that public sector organizations are usually more resistant to tough messages from independent quality assessors, more resistant to admitting they may have been mistaken. That could reflect genuinely greater barriers to getting approval for change; their greater complexity of role and diversity of stakeholders; or more bureaucracy to overcome; but the bar is apparently harder to jump over for public sector bodies. That is unfortunate for all of us.

Finally to one issue around self-assessment that we have never been able to crack so far, publication. There is absolutely no doubt that one of the most potent drivers of better performance in England in the past 14 years has been prompt publication of independent inspection reports. In the early years from 1993, the running was made by the schools inspectorate, Ofsted. Ofsted involved children's parents in inspections and took pains to ensure that at least a summary of their inspection report on each school was in those parents' hands too. The result has been a surge in 'parent power' in public sector schools, similar to that in private fee-paying education. Parent interest drives schools to achieve more. Stories abound of parents of very young children moving house to fall into the locality of the school they believe will be best later on. Ofsted's reports on the performance of local schools are routinely covered in local media, widening the circle of interest to people who know the teaching staff and congratulate them or commiserate with them, further adding to the incentives to do well.

Adult learning caught up in 1998 when we introduced primary publication of independent reports from, first, the Training Standards Council and then the ALI, on the internet. Even if a company subcontracted out its training, the company name appeared at the head of the report. Its responsibility for what was done in its name was absolute and inescapable. We had occasional queries about the fairness of this. They included a transatlantic discussion with an American agricultural equipment manufacturer concerned that the poor showing of its UK subsidiary in delivering staff training would discourage customers. But, in the end, nobody disputed that what we were doing was right. Nobody sued. Everybody accepted that what the world knew had to be acted upon.

The same arguments have to be compelling in relation to self-assessment. In our country, self-assessment reports are a conversation with other professionals, in funding agencies and inspectorates. As we suggested at the beginning of this chapter, the result is that very few providers volunteer to put their heads into the lion's mouth. If they can persuade funding agency contract managers that they are doing better than the independent assessors eventually find is justified, then the funders have, to some extent, been made complicit in continuing to support underperformance. There is no great reward for being honest in self-assessment.

The case is altered by publication. There the public could easily contrast four years of self-aggrandizement with a poor independent assessment report. It could readily be made contractually compulsory to publish a sequence of self-assessment reports alongside independent reports. An easy comparison of grades would help keep self-assessment realistic. There is some hope, as we write, that a new quality measure, the funding body Framework for Excellence, will make publication a mandatory requirement. If it happens on schedule, in autumn 2008, it will be a major step in making self-assessment credible.

We strongly recommend that countries new to our methods publish self-assessments, from the outset. You will discourage the dialogue between self-assessment and independent quality assessment from slipping into gaming. That is a prize that no national system and no provider anxious to excel could ignore.

Case Study 5 .

JHP Training: quality means profitability

JHP Training is one of Britain's oldest and largest work-based training providers. It is owned by the Pitman family whose ancestor invented one of the earliest worldwide office techniques, Pitman shorthand notation. Today's business was founded in 1983. The company employs over 500 staff in 50 centres across the UK. At any one time it has more than 6,000 learners on programmes in several areas of learning. It works with the two major British funding bodies, a host of private companies, and has innovative training schemes such as that for young mothers-to-be working towards the Duke of Edinburgh's Awards.

In the late 1990s JHP Training was suffering in a tough marketplace. Employers had cut back investment and the quality of training was hard to maintain. A new managing director accurately identified the problem: 'I started to tell our people that the better we do, the better it is for our bottom line. If we do a bad job, we won't get paid for it.' A concerted drive to increase quality and profitability hand-in-hand began with the turn of the new century.

A five-year development plan was halfway through when JHP Training was independently assessed by the ALI in 2002. ALI grades matched those which JHP had proposed in its self-assessment, confirming that the company was taking a realistic view of its position. 'We didn't want to fool ourselves.' While JHP achieved satisfactory grades overall, it was weak in quality assurance and in its important retail area of learning. As the managing director noted, 'That ALI first inspection confirmed that we had to pay more attention to detail and set up a proper quality system.'

A partial ALI reassessment in 2004 confirmed that JHP had made good use of the directions for change that it had been given. A new intranet had significantly improved internal communications, ensuring that staff in the regions could easily check whether they were following a company procedure or policy. Consistency of operation increased. The widespread adoption of electronic communications also made the company lighter on its feet, more able to bid quickly and successfully for contracts. A much more delegated management structure allowed what the managing director called the creation of 'a team of leaders at all levels, not a hierarchy. We have to make sure we are innovative enough to cope with change in the future.' While managers at the 50 centres were given greater freedom in making decisions and carrying them through, regional managers were encouraged to spend more time travelling among centres, distributing good practice. The commitment of centre managers to the health of the business was reinforced by ensuring that they were able to progress right through to the most senior levels of the organization. Staff retention improved, cutting the costs of recruiting and training new people. The senior operations manager of JHP is one of its former trainees.

ALI independent assessments were able to work with the grain of a company already determined to achieve continuous improvement. The managing director summarized the relationship: 'Working with the ALI has helped us to reinforce the changes we had already made across the board. It has helped us to produce a better performance culture. Another thing the ALI has definitely taught us is don't stray into occupational areas you don't know anything about. You can diversify too much. We don't want our sales people to promise the earth if we can't deliver. We specialize in what we can do well.'

Ever since it began its programme of improvement, JHP Training has been profitable. Higher quality has led to profits and investment, creating a virtuous circle of business development.

Notes

1   *Annual Report of the Chief Inspector 2003–04*, Adult Learning Inspectorate, www.ofsted.gov.uk, Publications and research, Archive ALI
2   Heifetz, R A and Linsky, M (2002) *Leadership on the Line – Staying alive through the dangers of leading*, Harvard Business School Press, Cambridge, MA

6

Using data

When providers ask us which three things will most quickly boost their quality, we recommend 'Data, data, data'. As we described in the last chapter, there are many organizations awash with information which they do not use to drive continuous improvement. It is information plus intelligent analysis and application that we mean by 'data'.

So far as the improvement of learning is concerned, a breakthrough in defining useful data was made by our friend Barrie O'Sullivan at the Audit Commission in the UK more than a decade ago. This was the definition of a single learner 'success rate', integrating both retention on a programme of learning and achievement of whatever goal was selected as the desired result.

$$\text{Success rate } (\%) = \frac{\text{Number who successfully completed the programme}}{\text{Number of learners who started the programme}} \times 100$$

Taking a very simple example:

$$\frac{50 \text{ successful completers}}{100 \text{ starters}} = 50\% \text{ success rate}$$

The reason that this modest formula is so powerful is that it stops providers manipulating either of the key variables, retention and achievement, in order to present the most favourable account of their work. For example, where only achievement is measured, as it is in the English

GCE A level, the temptation is for schools to prevent those learners whom they think are likely to fail from entering the examination. If you only measure achievement it is possible to so arrange things that your achievement rate will be close to 100 per cent. If, to take another case, retention is regarded as an 'in-year' measure rather than covering the whole duration of a programme of study, learners on a two-year programme, for example, whom the provider thinks are unlikely to achieve, can be dropped or transferred to another course of study at the end of the first year. Such practices make the provider look good but are not necessarily in the best interests of learners. They fail our basic test that quality should be measured as the extent of benefit to learners. Both these practices are possible within our national system and we have seen examples of unscrupulous manipulation.

COOKING THE BOOKS

Perry published some realistic examples in the ALI monthly newspaper, *Talisman*, showing how essentially the same learner performance could lead to apparently very different public perceptions of providers' success, according to the convention used in particular sectors of learning or for particular kinds of examination:

- A hundred pupils at a school start on a two-year programme of three GCE A-level subjects. At the end of the first year, 80 are left. Early in the second year, 60 are entered for three A-level examinations, 10 for two and the remaining 10 for none. Of the 70 entered, 58 achieve three A-level passes at various grades, some of which have little use for progression to university. The 10 who attempted two subjects all succeeded. The apparent success rate is 97% (68 out of 70) and the school presents itself as a very high performer, effectively ignoring the outcome for the 42 pupils who did not achieve what they hoped for at the outset and the results of those whose grades were too low for university entry.
- At a further education college, 100 students start on a two-year national diploma programme on 1 September. By 1 November, 80 are left and they are counted as the 'entry cohort' under funding body

rules. Of that 80, 70 remain until the end and take the examination and 58 pass. The apparent success rate is 70% (58 out of 80), a very respectable result which takes no account of the 20 learners who left in the first few weeks.

- At a work-based training provider, 100 learners start a two-year apprenticeship on 1 September. Over time, 42 drop out or complete only those aspects of the apprenticeship that they need to prosper in their jobs. The apparent success rate is 58% (58 out of 100); satisfactory, but, on the face of it, reflecting far less well on the provider than do the same outcomes, differently presented, at the school or the college.

In every case, 58 of the 100 learners who started out achieved what they wanted at the beginning. Three different, entirely legitimate, conventions produce achievement rates of 97 per cent, 70 per cent and 58 per cent, respectively. Once statistics of this kind become rooted in public consciousness, it is politically very difficult for governments to get away from them. They probably fuel a wholly unwarranted complacency among the providers that do well out of a particular convention but it will be very difficult for our own government suddenly to change the presentation rules for school GCE A-level results, for example. If the 97 per cent school success rate in our illustration becomes 58 per cent like the work-based learning provider, even though arguably this would benefit learners by giving them unbiased information, the challenge of securing a well-informed media response to the change might cause political mayhem.

Success rates should present the real prospect that those who start out on a course of learning will succeed in the end. For that reason, we would urge those countries that have a realistic choice in the matter to adopt the pattern we recommend. It is in nobody's interest, in fact, if providers are able to 'cook the books' by misrepresenting, within the rules, the level of benefit they offer learners.

There are some genuine dilemmas to be faced, however. The work-based training provider in our example operates the purest form of integrated success rate. If a learner decides at the end of the first day that an apprenticeship in hairdressing is the wrong career move, it might represent a 'failure' in the success rate data. That is one of the reasons why achievement levels in work-based learning can appear catastrophically low, even where the provider is doing a reasonable job. There is a respectable argument that a 'period of grace', something like that shown in our example of a further education college, should form part of a scheme of data presentation and this has now been accepted in England. Whether it should be two months long is debatable, but some kind of 'taster' or trial period, outside the official statistical returns, is likely to benefit learners and providers alike. It would not compromise our mantra that benefit to learners should be the central consideration in all decisions. To fulfil its potential, the content of an induction period should clearly be rich enough to give learners a fair sample of the experiences they will have in the rest of the programme. It should also assist the provider to make a well-informed analysis of whether the learner is suited to that programme. Those things are good in themselves, avoiding the waste of everyone's time, effort and goodwill, as well as allowing a proper statistical account of the reality of adult learning.

To be seen on equal terms with the further education college and the work-based training provider – the latter with a 'period of grace' in its learner entry data, the same as the college – the school would have to make some major changes. If a learner's aim was university entry, their declared achievement goal would have to be something like 'three GCE A-level passes at grades A*–C'. Only the proportion of those who were present at the end of the agreed induction period and who eventually attained three A*–C grades would count in the success rate. In our country, a treatment of statistical data of that kind would probably reduce the number of learners taking academic courses and divert them towards vocational programmes, which might be more beneficial to our success in the global economy. Such is the power of data, if the politics of state-aided learning allows us to harness it.

SEEING IS BELIEVING

A good thing about a single, primary indicator of a provider's effectiveness is the ease with which it can be monitored by managers. Changes and trends are easy to spot. Let us give you a simple example of the importance of presenting vital data in a graphic way, albeit one from a different activity in the assessment of learning. At the Training Standards Council we made a significant mistake in configuring the reports production process. The result was that we fell behind our fairly unambitious schedule of publishing an inspection report within 12 weeks. As every manager knows, once you have done something stupid, it takes a complex of remedies to get back on track. One important part of that is getting everybody committed to digging you out of the mire; they have to be able to see the problem the way you see it.

We had been recording the time it took to publish each individual report. When that report eventually went out it was ancient history. Nobody but the editors loved it any more. The inspectors and managers whose job it was to cooperate with the editors to turn round queries and accuracy checks quickly without busting the production schedule had all moved on to new, fresh, shiny things. The solution lay in the fact that we carried out inspections and published reports at a constant rate throughout the year. If we put up a chart in the office that showed 20 inspections completed this week and 20 reports published, it did not matter that this week's reports did not cover this week's inspections. The fact that the numbers matched meant that publishing was keeping up with inspecting. If the reports production line on the chart dropped below the inspection line we were falling behind our 12-week schedule. If it rose above it, we were all doing well and beating our schedule. Hooray! A glass of champagne all round.

That simple device not only got everyone behind the effort to catch up, but it also helped us see more clearly how we could improve the production flow and enabled us to set and reach a new, six-week, publication target. That is the power of well-chosen data presentation.

Adapting this technique to the goals of the individual provider, the integrated success rate can very easily be shown on a chart, helping staff who support different steps in The Learner's Journey to pull together to achieve a common end.

GETTING BEHIND THE NUMBERS

Let us say that managers see the beginnings of a falling trend in the success rate. That is the moment when learners' achievements and retention need to be disaggregated and each one checked out in detail. Learners are dropping out early. How early? Is it to do with confusing marketing so that people become disillusioned as soon as they start? Is it to do with a clumsy interview process that misleads, or does not enquire about motivation and aptitude with enough thoroughness? Is it about a boring, process-focused induction, which gets our learners informed about the curriculum, the assessment regime and health and safety at work, but convinces them at the same time that they want to be anywhere but here? Are we putting people on the wrong programmes, in terms either of subject or level? Do we have a member of staff who is incompetent or abusive? A well-conceived dataset will open up a way into those questions. It will not necessarily answer them but it will show you where to look and prompt you to probe the right issues. The questions in this paragraph relate only to the first few steps in The Learner's Journey. The same kind of potential concerns and questions relate to every step and, wherever possible and appropriate to the scale of the organization, data that can throw light on them need to be collected.

What are the kinds of questions, related to relevant aspects of The Learner's Journey, that we might want numerical measures to help us understand?

Recruitment	How many enquiries do we receive?
	How many applications?
	How many places do we offer?
	How many successful applicants accept a place?
	How many take up their place?
	Were there differences among all these data according to gender/race/age/ prior experience/disability?
	What do we spend to recruit each person who starts a programme?
Induction	How many new entrants undergo induction?
	How many complete the induction process?
	How satisfied are new recruits with each specific aspect of the induction process?
	What does induction cost?

Initial assessment	How many recruits undergo initial assessment of their capabilities achieved through prior education and experience?
	How many drop out or are redirected to other programmes/providers?
	What does initial assessment cost?
Teaching and learning	What are the teaching observation grades?
	Do learners' attendance and punctuality records suggest that they disfavour particular teachers?
Reviews and assessments	How long does it take learners to reach each stage of competency?
	How many pass/fail intermediate assessments?
	Are there differences according to gender/race/age/prior experience/disability/ teacher/assessor?
Achievement	How many achieve each qualification/grade/distinction/unit/subject?
	Are there differences according to department/subject/teacher/assessor?
	Are there differences according to gender/race/age/prior experience/disability?
Progression	How many progress to relevant employment/ a higher award?

A FOCUS ON OUTCOME

These questions help measure The Learner's Journey, its degree of sure-footedness, its speed, its outcomes. Sometimes, the process is seen as a pipeline. A company training people to take up a new business opportunity, for example, will express the outcome as job-ready employees arriving to start the work, with very careful measurements taken at every stage along the pipeline to ensure that they progress smoothly, quickly, reliably and cost-effectively. That can be a useful conceptual tool; seeing everything from a perspective of desired outcome and the removal of blockages to progress. It can help eliminate process-dominated thinking through which a recruiter, for example, might see the job as packing in entrants at all costs, regardless of the probability of their achieving outstanding outcomes. Pipelining emphasizes efficient progression, to the benefit of employer and learner alike.

Let us give you an example where pipelining might help. In the UK, welfare-to-work programmes are offered by the government agency, Jobcentreplus. Not much ambiguity about the desired outcome there. Jobcentreplus programmes, the New Deals, Workstep, are about getting people into sustainable employment in the belief that this is the very best way of restoring an adult's self-respect and choices in life and removing them and their dependants from poverty. All the evidence suggests that is true and that the more quickly people get into work and out of a welfare scheme, the better it is for them.

There would be no difficulty in achieving that in a prosperous country if everyone had the necessary job-skills. Manifestly, they do not. A very few may be genuinely unemployable because of very severe disabilities or illness. More will have left school without the necessary knowledge even to begin acquiring job-skills. More still will have been in undemanding jobs and lost them, only to find that the globalized world has moved on and, without re-skilling, there are no job prospects left.

For all those good reasons UK welfare-to-work programmes contain learning options. Many people sign on to the New Deal, receive some good advice and support and go straight back into work. Some spend a great deal longer learning basic skills and new work-skills. Those are often taught in the same providers that offer free-standing courses of learning. A potential conflict arises instantly. Is it desirable that someone leaves a course of study part-way through and goes back into a job? It may well be if jobs are the prize. This is where pipelining helps to keep everyone's eye on the same objective.

COMPARING SIMILAR THINGS

Data related to The Learner's Journey need to be broken down according to occupations or subjects. There is obviously little scope for useful comparison where an employer or training provider operates in only one area – hospitality or construction or childcare, say – but wherever a provider offers multiple areas, contrasts drawn out from the data on each one can be revealing. This is a way to detect good practice and to test whether its application to another area is having a beneficial result.

Perry developed 'areas of learning' in 1998. In her original scheme there were 14 of them. Further refinement involving other organizations led to the introduction of a modified set of 15 areas of learning in 2005:

Area 1   Health, public services and care
      2   Science and mathematics
      3   Agriculture, horticulture and animal care
      4   Engineering and manufacturing technologies
      5   Construction, planning and the built environment
      6   Information and communications technology (ICT)
      7   Retail and commercial enterprise
      8   Leisure, travel and tourism
      9   Arts, media and publishing
      10 History, philosophy and theology
      11 Social sciences
      12 Languages, literature and culture
      13 Education and training
      14 Preparation for life and work
      15 Business administration and law.

There is plainly an element of pragmatism in forming these groups. They may not match the needs of every country. To some extent the groupings were made in order to build up reasonably equal volumes of work in the routine of the Training Standards Council so that we could make significant judgements about quality and trends after each year's inspections. While the subsets within 'Agriculture, horticulture and animal care' probably have worldwide application, the inclusion of 'cleaning, security' and 'public services' such as fire-fighting and policing in 'Health, public services and care' may not work well everywhere. The intention was and is to gather sufficient volumes of reasonably similar subjects and occupations together, to derive data to help compare, contrast and improve across a large college, for example, or a country.

We have already warned of the dangers of just collecting statistics and doing nothing useful with them. Data are stimuli and guidance to help managers take effective action, to make changes happen. The obvious way to make sense of the numbers is by using ICT, but this is not essential. When computers are used, nothing more exotic than a Microsoft Excel spreadsheet is needed to produce the necessary presentation and analysis. A great deal can be done with intelligent use of pen, paper and a pocket calculator in the service of well-informed curiosity. The same human faculties need to be in play, however simple or advanced are the means for crunching the numbers.

In further education colleges, for example, where most learners enrol early in the autumn after the summer break, it is fairly easy to cluster learners in year groups or 'cohorts'. The pipeline record for the 2008 entry cohort on a two-year programme will run its course for most learners in 2010, with an extension to 2011 to account for retakes among those who initially fail to achieve the award. In circumstances like this, simple tables can be drawn to show up success rates and the points where learners leave early.

Things are a little more difficult where enrolment is possible on a 'roll-on/roll-off' basis, helping adults to start learning at whichever time of year is best for them. They are also complicated in work-based training where, once again, it is often possible to start work towards a qualification whenever you begin a new job.

The practical approach to dealing with this is to use a similar analysis of 'cohort progression' as we would apply more naturally to the traditional college. Put simply, everybody who starts a particular two-year programme with a provider some time in 2008 becomes part of the cohort of 2008, due to qualify some time in 2010 or 2011, with a possible extension to 2012. The argument that this is a reasonable approach is the same one we applied when trying to get our report publication process back on schedule. After a while, most learning programmes reach a steady state, with significant numbers of learners starting each year. The proportion who achieve on time can be analysed without difficulty. The fact that those starts and finishes each occur over a 12-month period and are then totalled up for the year to make a notional cohort is irrelevant to the usefulness of the data in helping to manage and improve the programme. The argument is often made that this approach is artificial, that it is not a faithful representation of the way the learning is delivered. That is true, but it *is* a faithful guide to the quality of learning and it is this we are trying to assess and develop.

Having created our cohorts, natural or notional, tables will show whether the programme is gradually getting better or worse or whether it is marked with the chaotic fingerprints of feeble quality management.

AN EXAMPLE IN DETAIL

The analysis of data is useful at a course or programme level. It can enable managers to understand fully what is really happening within a learner cohort. Consider this example. A provider runs an apprenticeship programme centred around training schools in three different areas of the country. Around each training school are clusters of employers who provide the workplace element of the apprentices' training programme. The training schools provide off-the-job elements including study skills, theory and any remedial work that may be necessary. Managers have the following headline data to consider:

Apprenticeship: 2004–06 cohort

	Totals	Centre 1	Centre 2	Centre 3
Enrolment	500	150	200	150
Completion	360	100	170	90
Qualifications and achievement	310	80	140	90
Success rates	62%	53%	70%	60%

From this general information it is clear that (for this cohort at least) each centre performs differently, especially in terms of their completion rates. Centre 2 has considerably better retention at 85 per cent (170 out of 200) than the other two centres at 66 per cent (100 out of 150) and 60 per cent (90 out of 150) respectively, and its success rate is also the highest at 70 per cent.

Looking beneath the data we can learn more about this difference. Let us say that Centre 1 is in an inner city environment, perhaps with higher levels of deprivation and a greater proportion of apprentices for whom English is a second language than the other two centres, which are in prosperous suburban communities.

When the data from Centre 1 are analysed in yet more detail, we might find that the majority of apprentices who left the programme before it was complete did so within a couple of months of the start. Why did they leave? Exit interviews, records of the first assessment and the induction questionnaires, taken together, might suggest that many of these apprentices did not settle down quickly. Their first assessment seems to have been the catalyst for leaving. Investigations into both the induction programme and the first assessment show why this might be. The induction period was rushed, several apprentices started after the main group and they missed a lot of it. The first assessment included a theory test in examination conditions which lasted for three hours, as well as a practical test. Pass rates for the theory exam were low. More than half of the group was set remedial work and given another examination to look forward to. The exit interviews included comments that those leaving felt 'overwhelmed' or 'out of my depth'.

The other two centres approached the first assessment differently, giving shorter, less formal tests which, together, gave the same information but gathered in a less school-like way. Many of the apprentices at all three centres were not high-fliers at school. They became apprentices to get away from classrooms, examinations and formal learning. The analysis showed that a more systematic approach to induction was needed. Lessons could be learnt by comparing assessment practices across the three centres.

Looking again at these simple data, we can see that Centre 3 has the lowest rate of retention of all the centres at 60 per cent, but it managed to get qualified all the apprentices who remained until the end. Going deeper, the retention pattern throughout the two years showed a slow, steady rate of drop-out until halfway through the last year, when there was a rush of leavers.

In our example, let us say that there are four large employers in this area who accounted for 75 of the 150 apprentices at Centre 3. Detailed workplace assessment and attendance records from the centre might show that the employers have all been booming and many of the apprentices have been promoted, moved to other areas of work or were just too busy to continue learning. We might ask whether the centre has been flexible enough in setting dates and times for all off-the-job learning sessions.

What is it that Centre 3 is doing so well to ensure that everyone who stays on qualifies? We can suppose that there are three members of staff at Centre 3 who deal with the apprentices; two are trainers and the other provides support and administration. Both trainers worked for local employers in the past and have thorough, recent knowledge of the industry and the pressures the apprentices face at work. They visit the apprentices at work and keep closely in touch with their employers. Feedback from the apprentices is wholly positive. They value the training and the personal support they receive from the team.

At the other two centres the trainers are less familiar with local employers and their knowledge is less up to date. They do not visit apprentices at work because there are assessors specially trained to do the job by the employers. Feedback from learners is patchy. Some say that the trainers are 'remote'. They cannot see the connection between learning at a centre and their work.

In these examples, which are typical in our experience, examination of the headline data provokes questions which can often be answered by drilling down deeper. The golden rules are:

- Collect the full range of data accurately and systematically.
- Look for patterns and anomalies.
- Use data to ask questions.
- Act on what you find.
- Believe what the data tell you.

One of the challenges of quality management is to know what to look for. There are very many variables, some of them probably easy to explain away. Problems start when you explain away something that is, in fact, a hint of early failure. For example, it might be right one year to account for an abnormally high level of early drop-out among learners with a variety of everyday reasons – illness, motherhood, a change of job, lack of money and so on. In the next year, however, the same apparent rationale might in reality be socially acceptable evasions used to cover up dislike for the programme. It is difficult, but essential, to be able to tell the difference.

In such a case, carefully conducted exit interviews, properly recorded, might well reach beneath the excuses. It is also helpful to set limits in advance to the key variables, any straying beyond them automatically prompting detailed enquiries and discussion by senior managers or a supervisory board. A common approach is to set acceptable deviations from a norm, plus or minus if appropriate, and to use a traffic-light indicator to alert managers when data show performance straying beyond them to a predetermined extent. If everything is going broadly as usual the indicator is green. A little out of kilter triggers an amber indicator to prompt careful monitoring, and further deviation a red indicator demanding remedial action. This simple technique helps prevent performance deteriorating too far before something is done. It helps prevent an individual deciding alone that unusual data can be tolerated, without proper scrutiny and agreement with others.

Good data management will not necessarily lead to great performance. However, without it, very few organizations of any size are able to detect and deal with their shortcomings methodically, or to isolate what they do supremely well and build on it. Data are the manager's friend. They can help pick up problems and opportunities early. They can guide the choice of action. They open up issues to quick understanding by a wider group of people or to fresh eyes. These are considerable virtues which no ambitious learning provider can afford to ignore.

Case Study 6

Toni & Guy: a cut above the rest

Toni & Guy is a worldwide hair and beauty business with franchised salons. The company bases its hairdressing on 14 classic Toni & Guy styles which have to be learnt by apprentice assistants to a consistently high level whether they are in London, Sydney or Los Angeles. An apprenticeship usually lasts two years spent mastering the craft and the necessary technical knowledge. Immediately before going to work in a salon, assistants attend a six-week finishing school at a Toni & Guy Academy, honing their approach to customer care and the most advanced techniques. This is a successful and self-confident company.

In 2001 the Toni & Guy Academy at Manchester, in the north of England, was awarded low grades by the ALI and declared inadequate. A new general manager found the experience 'Devastating. But we didn't walk away from it. We unpicked every-thing in that (independent assessment) report and built on it.' The extreme disappointment was wholly understandable in an organiza-tion with 40 years' experience, serving 20 very critical salons in the region. The determined, positive response was typical of organiza-tions that achieve continuous improvement.

By the end of 2002, the Academy had redeemed its failure and achieved satisfactory grades at re-inspection. Fundamental to the change was convincing the salons that off-the-job training at the Academy was valuable and that the closer fit achieved during the recovery period between daily work and the NVQ made it relevant. The initial thrust was to improve discipline: 'We were quite regi-mented in order to get things on track. We really tightened up on attendance and punctuality. If someone turned up late, we would send them back to the salon.'

The next step was to push on towards world-class levels of achieve-ment. It took another two years of concentrated effort and uncom-promising change.

There is a tightly defined contract between the Academy and the salons where on-the-job training takes place, setting out clearly the obligations of both. On that businesslike foundation was built warm collaboration, with frequent visits by Academy trainers and assessors to the salons and an intensive drive to train salon staff as assessors so that they could contribute more fully to the programme. In the beginning, even basic data such as the number of learners and their state of progress towards qualification were 'hit and miss'. A consult-ant was brought in to design and install a tailor-made management information system, to the specification of Academy staff. 'Every day, the numbers tell us what we need to do. If we see someone is very near the end (of their learning programme) we go to their salon and push for completion. We want them to move on.'

An enjoyable, busy, creative atmosphere is a key to the Academy's progress. Comprehensive initial assessment of each assis-tant's preferred way of learning leads on to use of superbly illustrated textbooks, videos, group-work, role-play, brainstorming, 'mood boards'; whatever is needed to enliven each person's enthusiasm and involvement. The Academy's leaders believe that there is no reason for any learning to be dull: 'They throw themselves into health and safety – a lot of laughing goes on.'

In 2004–05, the Toni & Guy Academy was one of only five work-based learning providers to achieve grade 1 across the board. It was among the 'best of the best'. The company's managers described their ALI independent assessment in terms that underlined its contribution to still more improvement: 'We really worked together with the inspection team and they had a level of occupational knowledge we could respect. They went out and spoke to employers, they saw the impact of our training in the workplace. The lead inspector was fantastic, asking intriguing questions that took the process to another level.'

7

Consequences

There is no point assessing quality if you do not act on the information you have gained. Any effective system of quality improvement has first to enforce action and second to help make it successful. That takes us to the second point of The Transformational Diamond: Assistance for weak but aspiring organizations.

Assistance needs a tight connection to Assessment in order first to launch change and second to confirm the early signs of improvement. Let us suppose that independent assessment has shown that a provider is inadequate to serve the reasonable needs of its learners. Inadequacy is defined as one-third or more of its areas of learning or its leadership and management at grade 4. Managers and staff will certainly be disappointed and probably surprised. In some providers they will disbelieve the judgement, feeling harshly treated and perhaps antagonistic to those who made it. Such a state of denial, understandable though it may be in human terms, cannot be allowed to persist. While it does so, learners carry on getting a raw deal and staff do nothing to put the organization on the road back to health. Their initial sense of shock needs quickly to be transformed into recognition that the criticisms made were well founded and that, with good sense and energy, they can put things right and build a more successful future.

In part, the solution to this problem is the provider's nominee, already described. If the news is bad, the nominee role comes into its own. The nominee will have heard all the debates, been able to see and test all the evidence on which unfavourable judgements were based. The task in the wake of quality assessment is to convince everyone on the provider's staff that they have been fairly treated, that the tough report is to be welcomed as a clear agenda for change.

If nominees have authority in their organizations, then while convincing people that they can make something positive out of unwelcome news is an uphill struggle, they are well placed to be the strong right arm of managers in making improvements. We have seen many people start out as nominees, make a spectacularly good job of it and become inspectors or national figures in quality improvement, their experience sought everywhere.

DRIVING HOME CHANGE

But a good nominee is unlikely to be enough. At the Training Standards Council and the ALI we required reassessment of poor providers within about a year of the original declaration of inadequacy. A year is about right as a period of grace to achieve at least satisfactory performance. Much less and nothing of real significance can be done that has the wholehearted support of everyone in the organization. Taking everyone along is at the heart of culture change and it is culture change that is likely to be required. Much more and yet another intake or two of learners suffer a poor experience, and the sense of urgency, or perhaps better, emergency, is lost. The argument that a year is too short to make a difference has some merit, in that it is unlikely that there will be solid evidence of improved learner achievement in that time. The quality assessors are likely to be looking for signs of good intent and early indications of change, rather than reassuringly better achievement statistics. However, on balance, we believe a year before reassessment to be fair to everyone concerned: learners, the provider and the independent assessors who have to secure solid evidence of improvement.

A colleague at the ALI contributed greatly to the effectiveness of reassessment by converting it from an event into a process. Reassessment in its earliest form was an occasion for redemption or 'sudden death'. A provider would work away at the issues in the inspection report, in the hope of doing the right thing. Feedback from providers suggested this was inefficient. A great deal of effort could be wasted, not least when providers replaced things they did well in a paroxysm of change for change's sake. While some reassessments, those triggered by a declaration of inadequacy, required that the whole organization be re-evaluated, many dealt with a single area of learning. In that case, cool consideration of the strengths of other areas and their adaptation to reinforce the weak area is needed, rather than a general flurry of activity.

For that reason, to guide and modulate change in the lead-up to reassessment, the ALI introduced a series of interim visits; between two and four in the year. Having reduced the delay between initial assessment and publication of the report to six weeks or even less, steady momentum could be maintained throughout the year. The process began with a planning meeting, where the independent assessor chosen to carry through the reassessment process visited the provider. This took place within a month of publication of the report and concentrated on the provider's plans to improve, addressing the issues arising from independent assessment. As part of the process, the lead assessor assigned approximate timings to the interim visits and a preliminary focus for each one. What will we evaluate in three months' time, what in six and so on? This procedure gave providers the security to plan change in detail and on a steady schedule. Process, not panic. The dates set for interim visits imposed deadlines for each piece of work. A satisfactory interim visit, although progress was not 'signed off' in the sense that a new grade was assigned to part of the provider's work, offered reassurance that the changes were on the right track.

As we have insisted with all the procedures described in this book, an interim assessment visit and the initial planning meeting need to be summarized in both oral and written feedback. The Quality Assessment Framework should apply. Good practice in feedback should apply, with nothing in the brief, written summary sent to the provider immediately after the visit that has not been said face to face. In part, the reassessment process is concerned with rebuilding the confidence damaged during the initial, unfavourable assessment. It is about winning the trust necessary to help organizations change. Without it, nothing of lasting value is likely to be accomplished. The interim phases of reassessment are, in essence, a process of mentoring, guiding and confirming progress and blocking off wrong turnings before time is wasted.

The self-assessment process is important in tracking and evaluating progress. It can help providers to give a clear, authoritative account of themselves at these interim visits, setting out what has been done and their own judgements on whether it is proving helpful. It gives providers a reawakening sense of control, of taking responsibility for improvement rather than making change because someone else has forced the issue.

Effective interim visits are likely to be challenging. The lead assessor may well bring along others with specialist expertise in particular areas of learning or management. They look at work, interview staff and learners, seeking to know what is really going on to confirm, ideally, that the provider's beliefs and judgements about progress are solidly based. As a result, it should be possible to mark steps forward on the provider's improvement plan. In this way, the changes begin to take on a life of their own, each one building on the last and rewarding those people who made the difference.

Where this process works well, the final reassessment visit should hold few fears and no surprises. Certainly, the rigour and coverage of reassessment, where this involves all the provider's work, will be little different from the initial assessment a year before. Everyone in the provider will be involved. Everyone will have work to do to ensure that they represent themselves and the organization properly. Everyone will have anxieties, which will be resolved in the end, it is to be hoped, in the sense of accomplishment and jubilation of having transformed the quality of their work. There will be a new report and new grades on the internet.

CONFIRMING PROGRESS

Nor is it to be supposed that only a small step forward can be taken in a year, from grade 4 on our scale to grade 3. It is, in one sense, enough to be judged 'satisfactory' but it is scarcely satisfying. And, indeed, we have seen many, many providers that have risen from inadequate to good in a year, and a few that have become outstanding. This is an extraordinary achievement and one we have always celebrated as such. What it shows is the power of The Transformational Diamond to raise performance dramatically and fast. It could be argued that reassessment, the strict timetable and the possibility of another failure and probably the loss of livelihood that would go along with it are a big stick to beat providers with. The use of interim visits and mentoring by an independent assessor transforms further punishment into a fresh start; a real opportunity to break out of a mediocrity which may well have been long established. Most people know when they are just getting by, when the organization they work for is passable but not very good. The opportunity this approach gives to achieve a new status in which everyone can take pride is one not to be missed. It is not punitive. It gives a new priority to the drive to excel.

Completing our process-rather-than-event approach was a scheme of monitoring visits. These were made to providers that had once been inadequate but had recovered at reassessment, and also to those that were just about satisfactory at initial assessment; those that might have been described as coasting. Quality monitoring was not inspection in any formal sense. No grades were involved, no published report, but it did require that up-to-date achievement data and the most recent self-assessment report were sent to the ALI in advance. This was a means of tapering down the previous level of independent intervention in most cases, returning the provider gently to normal.

It was also used to check the state of providers that had undergone very substantial structural change – a takeover, perhaps, or rapid growth from one site to many – to ensure that learners were still being well served. The ALI provided a watchful presence in the background, guaranteeing first and foremost the welfare of learners. The essence of this procedure was that the focus of the visit could be determined by the provider itself, seeking advice and independent judgement about a subject of its concern. Between three and five themes could be chosen for a monitoring visit, some by the provider and some by the two independent assessors. They offered a means to keep improvement going or head off any backsliding. Monitoring is essentially a small-scale activity, guiding and stimulating without disrupting, but ensuring that the whole national system keeps moving forward.

THE HELPING HAND

What happens if a provider is lost? What happens if the result of independent assessment was such a shock that its staff have no idea what to do next? This is unusual but not rare. It can be the fault of the provider itself. It can also be the result of a new learning programme, perhaps imposed by government for good and urgent reasons, so urgent, maybe, that too little preparation was made.

One such example was the 'Workstep' programme in our country, a much-needed preparation for people with disabilities to secure a mainstream job. The potential for their employment has risen enormously in recent years, with wider appreciation in society in the UK; ICT, in particular, extending the reach of people with disabilities; and globalization raising the urgency of deploying every capable person. The providers that took on Workstep were often among the very best; organizations with decades of experience in serving disabled people, often through using sheltered workshops where simple manufacturing could take place without some of the hurry and pressure of a fully commercial environment. Many of them failed abysmally under the new demands of Workstep, with its emphasis on helping people leave the permanent protection these providers had once offered. They were awarded grade 4 after grade 4, to the satisfaction of nobody. To carry on in this way, repeatedly confirming failure without exploring the reasons and remedying them, would have been the approach imposed by the limits of traditional inspection, but it obviously did not suffice in this case. The problem was nobody's fault; simply the result of the relentless change endemic in the globalized world.

The solution to this dilemma and to that of the puzzled provider was the ALI Provider Development Unit; the core of Assistance in The Transformational Diamond.

The Provider Development Unit (PDU) was controversial. It was suggested by a government minister demanding direct action to pull back failing providers from the brink. There was, nevertheless, a good deal of nervousness about the potential for conflicts of interest. The power of independent assessment as offered by organizations like the ALI lies in their perceived integrity. If there are grounds for providers or the general public to suspect that independence is compromised, that the organization is working to an agenda other than its own and other than that it has declared openly in its inspection framework, then its utility is gone. The most obvious conflict of this kind is personal, where an independent assessor may have some undeclared connection with a member of the provider's staff or may have worked for a rival organization in the recent past. Conflicts of this kind are fairly easy to guard against by imposing a contractual obligation on independent assessors to declare them and by offering providers the opportunity to raise concerns about assessment team members as soon as they are chosen and notified. It is essential that everyone trusts the disinterestedness of the team and it is right that legitimate challenges should not only be allowed, but welcomed.

With the PDU, however, a different kind of conflict might have been in prospect. What if the ALI were to judge providers inadequate in order to make work for its own staff in the PDU? It may sound a ludicrous concern, particularly in a government-funded body with no profit to be made from additional activity, no imperative for additional turnover, but it was a concern expressed by government and some providers alike.

It was addressed by separating the PDU from the ALI's mainstream quality assessment operation, sufficiently far to guarantee independence but not so far as to preclude the transfer of 'soft' information – the impressionistic data which cannot appear in a published report – which might help the PDU to help the provider. Initially 10 expert inspectors were seconded to the PDU for two years. They did no quality assessment work during that time. Their reporting lines within the organization were moved to a director other than those responsible for assessment operations. The effectiveness of the PDU and providers' responses to it were independently assessed by consultants. Everything we could think of was done to erect 'Chinese walls' – barriers to improper crossover of information and influence – between the PDU and its host organization, the ALI.

In practical terms, while the theoretical possibility of conflicts of interest remained, none were ever detected or complained of. On the contrary, the association of Assistance with Assessment was seen by providers from a very early stage as highly effective in dealing with problems which the quality assessment body, the ALI, understood more intimately than anyone else. Nobody but independent quality assessors has the opportunity to analyse the workings of an organization in such depth. With the PDU there was an opportunity to put that knowledge and understanding to good use, directly benefiting the provider and its learners. It was, for us, a seminal experience in helping form the model of quality improvement advocated in this book.

There was a second anxiety attending the birth of the PDU. There is a continuing tension in any free-market economy between those who believe that market forces alone will winnow out the weak and promote the best, and those who believe in some form of state intervention to help ensure this takes place. As far as the PDU was concerned, this adherence to market forces threw up two criticisms.

The first was that failing providers should be allowed to go to the wall so that other, better organizations could step in and fill the gap. We have no objection to that argument in principle. However, the example we have given, the Workstep providers, illustrates perfectly why principle does not always translate readily into practice. The failure was of many providers, not just one or two. They had already shown themselves to be excellent in a field in which there was no clamouring competition to take over their role; there was no 'market'. In fairness, also, the failure was not, at bottom, theirs. They were a symptom, not a cause. This, or something like it, is by no means unusual. There are many cases in which the provider, which independent assessment has just revealed in all its deficiency, is the only one around. It may be the only one to offer a particular, and perhaps relatively rare, occupational specialism in this or that part of the country. It may be a branch of an organization that does an excellent job elsewhere, the black sheep in an otherwise blemish-less flock. These and many similar reasons are enough to make hard-pressed contract managers pause before they allow the 'market' to lead them by the nose, at least for a while. The fallout of untrammelled operation of the market – the immediate need to find somewhere to transfer existing learners to, for example – is sufficiently daunting to make funding agencies hesitate.

Their hesitation can take the form of simply ignoring the findings of independent assessment. The problem is thrown into the 'too hard' file. Or, if a body like PDU exists, they can cooperate with it to give the weak but willing provider and its unfortunate learners a genuinely new start.

The second criticism, equally valid in principle, is that state bodies like the ALI should not offer services that could be sold by commercial consultancies. We have no problem with the essence of this argument either. However, it misses the point. The effectiveness of The Transformational Diamond lies in the closeness of connection between Assessment and Assistance, a closeness that cannot be readily achieved between separate organizations, we believe, without a risk of leakage of commercially sensitive or confidential information. Because of that major hazard, the links between analysis and remedy are likely to be more tenuous than is ideal. People hold back. We suggest that, while there can be no absolute proof that we are right, the success of the PDU will be enough to persuade most people to overturn the purist position in regard to free play of private companies. Indeed, our argument is that the existence of a body like the PDU, configured carefully in ways we are about to describe, contributes to the growth of the consultancy market. It is indisputably alive and well in the UK and internationally.

DEFINING THE PDU OFFERING

This is the PDU Assistance deal which meets the problems we have considered:

- separated structurally from quality assessment by 'Chinese walls', but within the independent assessment organization;
- staff seconded from assessment to assistance for an extended, fixed period, with no crossover between the two activities;
- assistance given free on the basis of a three-way formal agreement to cooperate, between the provider, its funding agency and the PDU;
- assistance absolutely restricted to 10 working days;
- a complete barrier between assistance and the re-inspection process.

Let us consider the three-way agreement first. Assistance cannot usefully be given to people who do not want to be assisted. We need to be sure they will play ball before we commit time and effort in trying to help them. Equally, it may be that the problems are within the powers of a funding agency to help fix; the help of contract managers is a necessary precondition for a rescue. One of the things that may be needed, for example, is investment. The assistance deal that works, we have found, is based on 'tough love' and on a common determination to put things right.

The provider will be distressed. It faces loss of its contract within a year if it does nothing. This is a major incentive but, in our experience, it is one best moulded to support a concerted effort to improve by specific, prior agreement on who is responsible for what. The responsibility of both the PDU, in our model, and the funding body is to assist the provider, not to take over its job.

The PDU promised to offer 10 days' free coaching, pointing the provider in the right direction as it made its plans to address the findings of independent assessment and carried them out. That entailed discussion; often an introduction to techniques for sorting out priorities; and guidance on developing a self-critical business culture. The funding agency promised to hold back from removing the contract and to help in any reasonable way it could to support the provider. The provider – formally – signed up to working energetically to sort itself out. The deal was that if the provider hung back, was awkward or reluctant in its relations with the other two parties to the agreement and in doing what it undertook to do after discussion with them, the PDU would withdraw and the funding agency would find another provider to do business with. It may have been Hobson's choice but it was a choice, nonetheless. The provider's responsibility to put its own house in order, to manage its business for the benefit of its learners was, if anything, sharpened by the Assistance agreement. It was emphatically not let off the hook.

The restriction to 10 days' assistance met the concern that the PDU might unfairly compete with private consultancies. Providers that have been found wanting often contract with consultants to help them out of trouble. Many do so on the rebound, without first coolly considering what they need to do to redeem themselves and who might be most qualified to assist. That is a bad start for both the client provider and the consultant. The provider is likely to waste money which it may sorely need for investment. The consultant is likely to be frustrated by the vagueness of the brief; perhaps by the gradual realization that their skills are not best fitted to the problem in hand; and the imminence of an unsatisfactory outcome. None of that is in anyone's interest. Better by far that the PDU help providers to pin down their development needs, paving the way for effective consultancy afterwards.

The PDU contribution was to help the provider fully understand the inspection outcomes which, in published form, will have been clear but necessarily compressed. It was to coax the provider into preparing a remedial plan which thoroughly addressed the weaknesses and built on the strengths. It was sometimes to give some basic business management and quality management training and occasionally very, very simple techniques to help separate the wood from the trees. Even SWOT analysis (Strengths, Weaknesses, Opportunities and Threats) has been shown anew to struggling providers on occasion. It was to introduce staff to self-assessment disciplines, helping everyone in the organization to regain control and confidence. It was certainly to act as the friendly insider; the person who had seen it all before and had seen worse outfits than this one get their act together and prosper. Done well, the job of the PDU adviser not only opened up the true potential of the provider and helped its recovery for the benefit of its learners, but it also reflected very favourably on the parent independent quality assessment body, the ALI. The PDU swept away the suspicion among providers that the job of the ALI was to find fault. The PDU made it abundantly clear that the endgame for the ALI was improvement and, even if the road was rocky, the ALI and the provider were striving towards the same end.

PDU advisers invariably grew close to the providers they helped. The relationship was like midwife and mother. Together they witnessed a rebirth. That the adviser stepped right back from any involvement at all with any stage of the re-inspection was therefore vital. The adviser was not neutral; the independent assessors had to be. The fact that each knew with absolute clarity that success for the provider and its learners depended on this contrast ensured that neither sought to blur it by inappropriate contact or consultation.

THE LEGACY

This approach was extraordinarily effective. Providers assisted by the PDU improved by an average of 1.06 grade points at re-inspection, compared with 0.88 grade points among those that had not been helped in this way. Well over 90 per cent recovered to reach at least satisfactory performance. Some would have recovered on their own. Given that the providers helped by the PDU were the very weakest, it is difficult to assess just how many. But the value to learners, the provider and its employees, the funding agency and the community more generally of not having to cope with the discontinuity caused by a collapsed learning provider was infinitely greater than the cost.

Let us return to the example of Workstep. The existence of the PDU attached to the independent assessment body broke the mould. It changed the paradigm from one where providers saw independent assessors as the opposition, however civilized and amiable, to one where providers, funding bodies and the ALI were all on the same side. Their common enemy was poor-quality adult learning. They needed no defence against one another. In those circumstances, the necessary first step in making Workstep a success was to underline that change, by bringing together representatives of the providers, the funding body Jobcentreplus, and the ALI.

It could have been a prickly encounter. In fact it resulted in amicable acknowledgement that *we* – all of us in common – had a problem. We all wanted the same outcome; fulfilled, independent living for people with disabilities. We all recognized the new imperatives for achieving that: globalization, wider job opportunities and better-informed attitudes in society and among mainstream employers. We were able to rebuild trust very quickly and agree a scheme to make Workstep a success. Assistance had now sometimes to precede Assessment; not to be offered as a response to failure. How crazy does it seem, when looked at rationally, that a learning provider could only get really effective help to excel as the result of failure?

The programme agreed consisted of training in the expectations associated with successful delivery of Workstep for funding body contract managers and providers; development of a clear understanding of independent quality assessment in these new, more complex circumstances among ALI staff; preparation of quality management manuals for the funding body; and deployment of the PDU whenever it was needed. It was not a quick fix but rather sustained capacity building and conversion. It heralded profound changes among charitable providers supporting people with disabilities, which led, among other things, to the reduction of sheltered employment by social companies like Remploy. The quality of Workstep provision rose gradually until, in 2006–07, the adequacy rate had risen to 67 per cent.

Direct assistance to providers by a branch of an independent quality assessment agency was entirely new. It aroused worries in England about conflicts of interest but none of these was realized in practice. The benefits in terms of quick, effective intervention which helped learners, funding agencies and providers alike were beyond all expectation for such an apparently simple move. The enduring changes, in terms of sustained improvement towards international levels of excellence and an utterly transformed relationship between providers and the ALI, were equally extraordinary.

In the next chapters of the book we will cover the other two facets of The Transformational Diamond which are similarly indispensable in changing a traditional safeguard based on the particular experience of the UK, inspection, into an internationally relevant quality improvement method.

Case Study 7

Cheadle Royal Industries: the PDU and a social industry

Cheadle Royal is a hospital for mentally ill people, in Cheshire, northwest England. Attached to it is Cheadle Royal Industries (CRI), a factory employing long-term hospital patients with help from a financial subsidy from the government 'Workstep' scheme. CRI has been in business since 1957, its principal aim being to offer people who would not normally be seen as able to hold down a mainstream job a paid therapeutic occupation in safe conditions. The factory makes paper party hats and decorations. Its products are inventive and well made, its service to customers excellent, but it cannot compete on price with items from China. A government subsidy, which once met 75 per cent of wage costs, by 2003 provided only 40 per cent and falling. The 'Workstep' programme incentivized releasing CRI workers to mainstream jobs, rather than their retention in sheltered employment. The average length of employment of staff at CRI was 17 years. CRI's world was turned on its head.

In 2003, ALI independent assessors awarded very low grades to CRI. A new manager at CRI and the regional 'Workstep' manager for Jobcentreplus asked for improvement support from the PDU. By that time, three months of the time allowed before re-inspection had already passed. CRI's action plan was huge – monstrous. The PDU adviser broke down all the procedures and audits needed into four areas: health and safety, equal opportunities, quality assurance and basic skills. 'We wouldn't have been halfway ready for re-inspection without that input. It helped us do things in the right sequence, not waste energy on the wrong things.'

While productivity among mentally ill workers was very hard to increase, concentration on key areas for employability and effective team-working helped CRI begin adaptation towards the demands of 'Workstep'. CRI's manager commented, 'Our people work at their own pace and we wouldn't dream of pushing them. If anything, they perform worse over time – it's a feature of their condition – and productivity declines. We walk a tightrope all the time. But we've all developed new ways of looking at the business, sat down and talked about everything and become much more aware.'

Part of the development required was improving routine procedures and safeguards to meet modern expectations. As CRI's manager noted, 'Most people think of us as super-safe.' However, there were no formal, written procedures for fire evacuation, for example, which would allow new staff to get quickly to grips with a basic safety requirement in a factory full of paper and feathers.

More demanding but even more vital in preparing workers for the possibility of mainstream jobs was help to improve their basic skills of literacy, numeracy and ICT. CRI's manager again: 'Our PDU adviser's favourite saying was "It's not rocket science." Well, finding someone who can deliver a Workstep-orientated programme of basic skills is. I could have got to the moon quicker!' The local Learning and Skills Council and chamber of commerce located a specialist and classes provided by a further education college were launched. CRI workers greatly enjoyed them as well as finding that they opened new doors.

At re-inspection in 2005 the independent assessors praised the 'good communications and effective leadership' and 'the good literacy programme'. The new grades were satisfactory, allowing CRI to get on with finding original and better ways to help give patients from Cheadle Royal Hospital more fulfilling and more independent lives. There is no blueprint for making progress in this work. It requires creativity and constant pressure on the presumed limits of disabled or ill people's capability.

Case Study 8

Learning and skills in prisons: training for good citizenship

The population of British prisons has risen rapidly in recent years with over 80,000 people now in custody, one of the highest proportions of national population in Europe. The majority are young men. Over 60 per cent of them are classified as functionally illiterate and 80 per cent are unable to write fluently. These very low educational levels result at least in part from the high correlation between early truanting from school and a life of crime. Most prisoners lack work-skills and the educational background to attain them easily. Over 60 per cent of released prisoners quickly re-offend. Government policy over the past decade has been to invest in their learning in order to reduce this figure but, until recently, prisons have been very poor at offering adequate opportunities. In 2004–05 over half of all occupational training and education in British prisons was judged inadequate. Just half of those had improved sufficiently when the prisons were re-inspected.

The problem was tackled nationally through ring-fenced funding which prevented prison governors from transferring the money away from learning to meet other priorities. It allowed long-term strategies to be adopted, including the appointment of a head of learning and skills to work directly with the governor of every prison. From the summer of 2005, the ALI was able to offer PDU support for failing learning and skills provision whenever it was needed. The response of the head of learning and skills at Featherstone Prison to a poor initial quality assessment by the ALI was typical: 'The rigour and focus of the process caught us totally unawares.'

Some of the areas on which PDU advisers most often concentrated were these:

- statistical data – often analysed and used so ineffectively that it was difficult for managers to evaluate performance;
- quality assurance – many prisons had few policies and procedures to assess and improve learning and those they had were seldom used effectively;
- self-assessment – widely misunderstood and underestimated as a means of achieving improvements;
- range of provision – many prisons missed readily available chances to give prisoners skills relevant to work outside and to accredit their accomplishments with qualifications which would help them get a job;
- individual learning plans – often seen as a bureaucratic chore rather than a scheme linked to each prisoner's sentence plan and intended to give relevance and direction to learning as inmates moved from prison to prison;
- course planning and management – seldom done in a way that made the most of investment and effort;
- sharing good practice – the closed, isolated communities in prisons hindered learning from successes and adopting them everywhere.

PDU advisers in prisons typically worked intensively with governors and prison officers to help integrate learning with the rest of the prison regime. The head of learning and skills at Dorchester Prison said: 'PDU support proved hugely beneficial. The visits of the PDU adviser kept us all focused and upbeat. They were refreshing and challenging, enabling us to take stock and prioritize actions quickly. One particularly pleasing feature is the continuation (after successful re-inspection) of a team-based, highly supportive approach to learning and skills throughout the prison.'

By 2006–07, the inadequacy rate for learning and skills in prisons had fallen to 16 per cent and all of those that failed at initial ALI quality assessment were satisfactory within a year, usually with the aid of PDU support. Learning in prisons is now seen as a mainstream activity, with an increasing number of companies offering employment in the latter stages of a prison sentence and to ex-offenders.

8

Building a national quality movement

We started the ALI with ambitions to make it an exemplary employer. With 100 people in a single office in the English Midlands, 150 more working out of their homes all over the country and nearly 700 associates, trained and ready for work on contract, the challenge of serving their learning needs equally well had us scratching our heads. The solution, we decided, was to set up a 'corporate university'; a network for all our staff. It would use blended learning methods – a mix of face-to-face and IT-based techniques – and would plan and record all their training so that it added up to something coherent and valuable for each person.

The corporate university movement is now worldwide, having started out in America. Typically, a big company discovers that, despite the very large sums of money and the time and effort it devotes to training and educating its staff, when questioned many of them say 'Training? No! Nobody ever gives us any training.' The first issue is to make people notice when they are learning.

You might observe that, in one sense, the fact that many do *not* notice is a good thing. It suggests that learning, developing new skills and acquiring knowledge are an everyday fact of business life. Growing on the job is a compliment to the good sense of the employer and the care that has been taken to design a job with some stretch and to match the right person to it.

But not noticing learning also causes some problems. At the national level it partly explains why governments and employers' representative organizations often bewail skills shortages, even when the economy is demonstrably coping well with the global market. That is sometimes the case in our country. A vast amount of knowledge and skills accomplishment is invisible to government and the metropolitan in-crowd. It leaves a trace in the national statistics only if it is partly paid for by government and if it leads to a nationally recognized qualification. Governments in democracies want to benefit citizens and to be seen to be doing so when elections come round. As a result, they often express learning targets in terms of qualifications, missing much of the unaccredited but economically valuable learning which is going on. Many also introduce schemes of assisted training which subsidize from the public purse learning which was happening anyway, paid for by private individuals and organizations. This kind of unrequested subsidy, this displacement, is criticized as 'deadweight'. In our country the presence of deadweight has been used as a basis to challenge the value of a number of programmes. They include the New Deal, support and learning opportunities for long-term unemployed people; and Train to Gain, a scheme used to give employers the money and help they might need to assist staff towards their first qualifications, shifting the initiative in learning from the 'supply side' (colleges and training providers) to the 'demand side' (individual employees and employers). These things all suggest a national anxiety, an anxiety which should not be ignored, to make learning noticed.

At the personal level, too, not noticing learning has some damaging effects. People often undervalue the contribution to their careers and wellbeing that their employers are making, perhaps causing discontent and resentment where none is warranted. If someone is unaware of what they have learnt, it is unlikely also that they are well placed to plan what it might be best to learn next. That can easily lead to unfulfilled potential and stunted ambition. No would-be winner in the global market can afford to let that happen on any extensive scale. Hence there is a growing movement in corporate universities and government adult skills programmes which seek to make learning visible, incremental and systematic.

We needed to learn from an organization that already had a successful corporate university and we chose Unipart; already the subject of a case study in this book.

As had Unipart, we rapidly saw that the corporate university idea could be extended well beyond our own employees and associates. What about all those people, probably another 2,000, who had acted as providers' nominees? What about the tens of thousands of others involved in self-assessment, workplace observation, quality improvement and management in those providers? What about the many more who worked as assessors and verifiers for the awarding bodies? All these people were not employed by us or directly connected with us but, as Figure 1.4 in this book shows, they are intimately involved in the same national enterprise.

We set about the development not only of a corporate university but also what we called, perhaps idealistically, 'the national quality community'. We chose a name for it – *Excalibur*. We settled on this partly because *Excalibur* contained the letters ALI but also because, associated as it is with one of the most powerful foundation myths of the English nation, the Arthurian legend, it would conjure up from people's subconscious minds the vision of the weak boy drawing the sword from the stone where the strong and powerful had failed. It spoke to everyone of the transformational power of ambition and self-confidence. It said that with courage and a little help from their friends, anyone could do anything.

We saw *Excalibur* – to mix metaphors horribly – as a road to improvement and fulfilment and as a semi-permeable membrane through which the things that the ALI learnt through independent quality assessment could be transmitted osmotically to the wider community of people committed to learning (Figure 8.1).

Excalibur formed much of the third facet of The Transformational Diamond: Accumulation of good practice. Its intention was to transfer knowledge and experience with all the vividness now possible with ICT. It was also to create circumstances in which the ALI enriched the adult learning and skills sector with what it knew, but did not dictate how the sector used it. We wanted to be at the centre of the circle, as it were, sending out good things to the farthest periphery, but we wanted also to

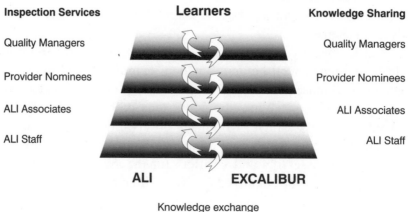

Figure 8.1
Source: ALI Corporate Plan 2003–06

encourage free radial communication between providers. We did not want to be a bottleneck, the only source of information and creative thought, but to help consolidate and disseminate what the sector as a whole knew in ways that would help others to be innovative.

It is hard, even now, to capture the excitement and even the grandeur of the idea. We believed that, through *Excalibur*, we could use the understanding we gained as independent quality assessors and, through the PDU, quality improvers, as tinder to light a bush fire. With a strong wind behind it, it would flare and spread determination to excel, the capability to do it and to help others do it. It would multiply our energies a thousand-fold.

This was heady stuff. In practice it was expensive to achieve and took a great deal of effort. But it worked. The main elements of *Excalibur* were these:

- well-produced instructional materials available free and, in most cases, both in hard copy and online for independent learning;
- face-to-face teaching with these materials, delivered by the ALI and others;

- an interactive online good-practice database;
- the 'Quality Champions Programme', a set of modular qualifications aimed at providers' nominees and quality management staff and based on reflective practice;
- an MA in quality assessment, aimed at ALI staff in the first instance but intended for eventual extension to providers and others.

The ICT platform was sophisticated and powerful, allowing the introduction of new services from time to time, keeping those that proved popular and abandoning those that did not. Needs come and go. Experiments in serving them are worthwhile, but inevitably some will not work or the demand will pass. Keeping up momentum, currency and freshness depends as much on dumping useless baggage promptly as it does on putting in more good things.

WHY *EXCALIBUR* worked

What we thought about *Excalibur* was obviously much less important than what users thought about it and did with it. For that reason, we commissioned a respected research consultancy firm, ECOTEC,[1] to evaluate *Excalibur* for us and much of what we say about it in this chapter is based on their findings. ECOTEC began its survey in September 2005, only a year after *Excalibur* was fully staffed and completely operational. The researchers consulted a large sample of learning providers, over 400 of them, as well as 11 major stakeholder organizations, including government departments.

For a service which was then almost new, the reactions were remarkably favourable. ECOTEC concluded that *Excalibur* 'clearly made a strong contribution to national quality improvement'. They found that both 'providers and stakeholders actively promoted and disseminated *Excalibur*, both within their own organizations and to networks of providers'. They reported that 'stakeholders and providers stressed that the link to the ALI – ensuring that all content is based on the findings from inspection – differentiated *Excalibur*.... This earns *Excalibur* its credibility, trust and respect.' The enthusiasm of the ALI's customers for the new service was confirmed by the fact that, even by October 2005, there were 34,000 visitors a month to the *Excalibur* website, not merely random hits but regular visits to check new material, each one lasting between 11 and 30 minutes on average. By 2006 over 90 per cent of learning providers agreed with ECOTEC that *Excalibur* helped build quality.

So what was it that made *Excalibur* so effective? The first point to emphasize is the one made by its users from the start and underlined in the association of quality assessment and improvement in The Transformational Diamond. *Excalibur* materials were those that the ALI's independent evidence had proved to work, to benefit learners, to help raise quality. There was nothing whimsical about the choice of good practice examples. They were those things that had withstood the evidential tests that the ALI threw at them and had been found to be so original and remarkable as to be worth sharing with other providers. As providers told ECOTEC, the values they associated with *Excalibur* were 'clarity and openness, as well as encouraging people to be positive about change'. Like the ALI itself, they felt *Excalibur* was 'not touchy-feely, warm and cuddly, but clear and stark (saying) "this can be improved".' One should only Accumulate what is worth accumulating and that is a hard-nosed business.

By helping all learning providers and learners, the ALI made clear through *Excalibur* that it was authoritative but not authoritarian. As we have said throughout this book, this is a vital distinction and one that cannot just be stated. It has to be proved. And once proved, the trust that underlies the power of The Transformational Diamond starts to grow. A work-based learning provider told ECOTEC: 'In the past ten years of development, (*Excalibur*) has got to be in the top three best things that have happened. One of the other two is ALI inspection in general.' We never did find out what the third good thing was.

The second key to the effectiveness of *Excalibur*, according to its users, was concentration. The fact that everything that the ALI had to say about any particular topic had been brought together in one place and described without jargon gave it added force. Useful information gathered into a one-stop shop is many times more influential in changing behaviour, in fomenting enthusiasm, than information which is scattered, accessible only with difficulty. A prison reported: 'Having the whole thing in one box has been helpful for self-assessment. Rather than having to rack your brains about what to do, *Excalibur* sets out a logical step-by-step outline of how to approach (it).'

Achieving this degree of concentration is partly a matter of the medium chosen to present the information. Electronic media are not just alternatives to printed material or face-to-face contact, they do different things. We learned from Unipart that very expert technical staff sometimes made serious, costly mistakes because they had forgotten simple skills learnt long ago. The use of a micrometer to check production tolerances is so basic a routine that it can easily be overlooked and then forgotten, with a consequent upswing in manufacturing rejects. Fixing that problem runs hard up against professional pride. A middle-aged engineer might reasonably resent being sat in a classroom and reminded how to use a micrometer but – as Unipart has proved – will contentedly use ICT to refresh basic skills discreetly and whenever necessary. No loss of face is involved. In a somewhat backhanded compliment, a provider interviewed by ECOTEC said that *Excalibur* suffered by 'not being a human being, so I can't talk to it' but came through with flying colours because 'it is there 24/7, 365 days a year, immediately available. (My PDU adviser) was excellent but she couldn't respond to e-mails immediately.'

The third central virtue of *Excalibur*, said providers, was its ability to involve all their staff. Everyone who is employed will have experienced the annoyance of a colleague being sent on a course to gather important information which they are supposed to 'cascade' to everyone else when they return. They never do. They are too busy catching up with the work that piled up while they were away. They quickly forget the excitement of being on the course. It was particular to the place, to the group of new people, as well as to learning new things. Anything they do pass on when they get back will be shorn of all that vitality. With *Excalibur*, everyone was able learn something fresh together, the office junior alongside the boss, because it was ICT based.

As a provider told ECOTEC, 'It has helped us to bring together all the information we need to use, and to involve our staff in self-assessment. It has helped us understand what the words mean and how everyone fits into the process.' In other words, *Excalibur* offered a democratic kind of information, giving everyone in an organization an opportunity to contribute fully. It was the rope on which everyone could pull.

These are the things users said were special about *Excalibur* information:

■ It was independently validated and authoritative.
■ It was concentrated, available in a one-stop shop.
■ It was open to all, a means of uniting everyone in an organization.

ACCUMULATING CORPORATE MEMORY

There is the makings of a simple rule of thumb here, suggesting what is needed to make Accumulation of knowledge and experience on a large scale possible:

$$\text{Accumulation} = \text{Validity} + \text{Concentration} + \text{Accessibility}$$

Let us give you an example of this equation in practice; one where use of a blended learning solution would have helped in creating Accumulation. The British Royal Navy provides sea training for the crews of warships from many countries. Warship crews change over often, keeping the vessel in service at sea while the more fragile human beings refresh themselves on land with their families. The crew changeover entails a very rigorous process called 'working up'. Week in, week out, exercise after exercise, every routine is practised to the point of exhaustion so that individual skills bind together to form an efficient new crew, capable of dealing instantly with anything the sea or hostile action might throw at them.

Once a week, every ship's state of readiness is assessed in a seagoing exercise called 'The Thursday War'. Surface ships manoeuvre together at action stations, while submarines attack from below and aircraft from above. Officers from the sea training group observe everything, praise or criticize as necessary, and eventually sign off the ship as ready for service. Working up takes several weeks.

All this works extraordinarily well. However, it might be further improved and speeded up if what was accumulated in the brains of the training officers could be made more easily available to all. Their knowledge is indisputably Valid. It is Concentrated. But it is not easily

Accessible, except through face-to-face contact. A database like *Excalibur* has the potential to reduce the time needed to achieve operational efficiency and therefore the period when a very costly piece of equipment, the ship, is operationally unavailable.

That, in the more peaceful context of most adult learning, is what we aimed for with *Excalibur*: to create a genuinely national stock of corporate memory and experience. The ECOTEC report suggested strongly that *Excalibur*'s users were convinced it worked. This is how. Let us take elements of *Excalibur* one by one.

INSTRUCTIONAL MATERIALS

We have stressed again and again that openness, sharing what you know, is central to the effectiveness of quality improvement. It is not always something that an organization with the force of government behind it finds easy to do. The old saying 'Knowledge is power' is deep-rooted. Those who have knowledge too often find that they enjoy the sense of power that secretiveness gives them. 'Open government' seems the most elusive of all goals. However, while going out of your way to share what you know may be counter-intuitive for some, it is the way that a whole organization or nation moves forward to global competitiveness.

We have given ALI materials to every British provider that asked for them. Airline baggage allowances permitting, we have done the same for everyone in other countries, apparently our competitors. That feels right to us. One world. We are all in the same, rather frail boat, dealing alike with problems beyond the solving of any one of us: global warming, terrorism and, optimistic though we are about it, the long-term effects of burgeoning global trade. Nobody knows what the future will be like. All we can do is to make our small contribution to its success.

And everywhere we have handed out our materials, people have been ecstatic. 'So clear! So easy to understand!' Their astonishment is not really so surprising. Sadly, most academics, most bureaucrats – and, reluctantly, we have occasionally had to admit to being both – are terrible communicators. So, banal as it seems, we perhaps need to go through what makes for good instructional materials.

First, they need to be written in good, plain English (or French or Thai or Urdu). The people who do it best in our country are usually journalists on high-quality publications. They use short sentences, avoid obscure words whenever they can and explain what they mean rather than assume a shared understanding of jargon. The secret is to read out loud what you have written. If the words that come out sound like they belong to someone else, or come from the more obviously robotic car satellite navigation systems, you are not communicating well. There is every reason why the language used to help people raise quality should be inspirational, lively and even beautiful.

What you must not do, particularly if you are in a position of authority, is to disguise the humanity and uncertainties you share with your readers. The emotion-shorn language of police communiqués may be alright for announcing shocking road traffic accidents or grisly murders. It is designed to create distance. It will not do as a means of helping others share what you know.

Second, design and production matter. In our country, certainly, official publications used to be austere. They were printed, without illustrations, in black ink on off-white, cheap paper. Sometime in the last decade, someone decided that the kind of graphic design values used in magazines or books were also appropriate to policy announcements. We made the same decision ourselves in 1997 when we produced a quality assessment framework called *Raising the Standard*, instead of following the line of the organization we had just left, which published FE Circulars 97/12 and 97/13 at much the same time and for the same purpose. Our publication sought to inspire from the moment you first saw it. The others were calculated to attract only the most determined, only those who had to know what was inside.

A key point is that when you start out to build a widespread community of interest in achieving excellence, you cannot know who will eventually prove influential in helping you do so. You have to entice everyone with a possible interest to join in. You cannot rely on a tight professional group, pre-selected and resisting entry to all others by virtue of their rarified understanding of impenetrable documents and language. If you produce instructional materials which look good, feel good and are deliberately made to attract all-comers, you will be well on the way to widening the circle of your collaborators. That is essential because the whole point of the exercise is to start off something unforeseen, something whose outcomes are far greater than your input: the 'bushfire'.

Lastly, a point which we continue to be uncertain about, instruction and materials given freely. There is a point of view in our country to the effect that people do not value what they do not directly pay for. The National Health Service (NHS) is often used as a case in point. It costs a great deal of tax revenue to deliver (very efficiently, in fact) a service which is free when you need it. It is possible that the ambiguous attitudes of British people to the NHS stem partly from the invisibility of their payment to support it. When questioned in the abstract they say that the NHS is the best thing government provides, remembering atavistically perhaps the hideous, painful, uncared-for old age which was common-place only two or three generations ago. When asked about the NHS now, they often say 'It's going to the dogs. Just look at the stories in the newspapers!' But when recounting recent, direct experience the story tends to be about wonderful care from doctors and nurses and no-expense-spared medical treatment.

The differences between perception and objective reality can be illogi-cal and puzzling. Both have to be managed effectively in an enterprise of this kind. Would we have got more commitment to our ideals by charging for materials and workshops and instruction? It is possible, but we decided not to, with the full support of our government.

Our reasons were these:

- We wanted everyone to join in; not just those who could afford to.
- The perception of our own organization we wanted to encourage was one of help willingly given.
- The fees and charges we would collect would, in many cases, be simply recycling public money given to providers by the state to buy training for others.
- In many cases, for example a subscription website, it would be expen-sive to collect the money.

Other countries and other kinds of quality improvement services may well take a different view. Looking at some of the ECOTEC user data, we occasionally wondered whether we might become the first adult learning dotcom millionaires if we had charged for *Excalibur* materials, but no. The intellectual property was, in fact, sourced from the people we hoped to share it with. It was theirs, codified and presented by us. It would have been wrong to charge for it, we felt, even though, once again, we risked all the accusations of anti-competitive behaviour from private training organizations and consultancies which we have discussed elsewhere in this book.

FACE-TO-FACE TEACHING

The reason why we did not alienate people who perfectly reasonably wanted to make their living from training trainers was that they, too, had the use of *Excalibur* materials. The prosperity of this secondary market in *Excalibur* training materials in fact added to the bushfire. Other people using our materials could achieve greater outreach than would have been either possible or desirable for the ALI itself. The ALI was an independent quality assessment agency. We could justify sharing what we found out from assessment for the common good, using more effective techniques than had been available before. We could not justify spending all our time on it, detracting from our core business.

Sometimes the judgements we had to make were difficult. We agonized when people whom we knew were neither public-spirited nor competent used *Excalibur* materials. Would this not devalue them? It is a reasonable anxiety but wrong. Common intellectual property of this kind is always being added to. It grows with every piece of new evidence and experience coming from independent quality assessment. It grows as national adult learning provision improves and changes. Whilst the uncontrolled use of *Excalibur* materials might well have sullied them sometimes, by associating them with poor presenting organizations – a fluke in the wind behind the bushfire, if you like – there was always more, always something fresh, coming from the source.

That is the kind of argument which is also made about the quintessential modern information and learning medium, the internet, and it has been proved right. Information is not of itself valuable. What makes it valuable is its application. Application, in the case of *Excalibur*, was in the hands of adult learning providers, where it should have been.

GOOD PRACTICE ONLINE

Efficient dissemination of the good practice developed by somebody so that it can benefit everybody is the Holy Grail of continuous improvement. If you make the rest as good as the best, again and again as what is best changes to meet new circumstances and gets better still, you will be world-class. Once, this was very hard to do. With the arrival of web-based dissemination, it is a great deal easier and cheaper. The Accessibility term in our equation can be tackled with some confidence, provided that Validity and Concentration have received and continue to receive the attention they deserve.

The *Excalibur* good practice database did something which is essentially simple:

- An original and very effective technique was revealed by independent assessment (Validity).
- It was described by someone knowledgeable enough to clearly express what was good about it and how it might be adapted for use by others (Concentration).
- It was posted on the *Excalibur* website, complete with contact details for the organization which developed the techniques in the first place (Accessibility).
- Other providers saw something in the example which would solve a problem for them or add value to their work, contacted the originator to explore the ideas in more depth, and adapted them for their own use, benefiting their own learners (Accumulation).

Perhaps needless to say, there are some conundrums to solve before it works well in practice.

Our experience is that, in the heat of an independent quality assessment, nobody has the time to record and analyse carefully an example of good practice. The best you can hope for is that it is noticed, it causes excitement, delight and celebration and it appears in one or two lines of the published report. If you coaxed them hard, independent quality assessors would also pass a brief note of what they had seen back to the *Excalibur* production team.

Good practice databases are not assembled by magic. They require ICT professionals to make them work and learning professionals to load them up with good things and keep them refreshed. They have to have enough examples on them, a minimum of 200 perhaps, to cover the range of different provision in adult learning. If there is nothing about prisons on a good practice database, for example, the probability is that prison learning staff will look no further. If there are one or two prison examples, they are likely to feel sufficiently encouraged to check what they might borrow from other sectors. The examples have to be changed regularly, staying on for no more than two years, with ideally eight or ten new ones coming on every month, tagged so that users know where to look for something fresh. These examples have to be interestingly presented.

Describing and presenting good practice examples is time-consuming. Once alerted to something worth seeing, we found that another professional had to go to the provider, by appointment, and explore the situation more thoroughly. We trained all those doing it to use a digital camera to something like professional standards so that they could shoot still photographs and short video clips to help describe the good practice example. It is often much better to see something done rather than work out what is going on from a verbal description. When they returned, they wrote up the example and presented it on a standard format.

There are pitfalls in the use of good practice. It is too easy for people who feel vulnerable to slavishly copy a practice which works well elsewhere, do it badly and create a bigger mess than they started with. It is essential to foster an attitude that enquires after the concept beneath the practice and then creatively adapts it to fit another set of circumstances. For that reason, *Excalibur* good practice examples included suggestions about ways that the idea might be modified to work elsewhere. This demanded imagination and broad experience on the part of the presenter. We do not want to narrow down the potential applications of an example of good practice by suggesting too prescriptively how it might be used, but we do want to stir people's creative juices so that they think through the process of adaptation. It is a fine line to tread and one that people need to be taught how to feel confident about. It is one of the reasons why arranging a visit to a provider to see some particularly good practice; going there, analysing and recording; and then writing up the example and putting it on the database takes something like three person-days' work. Two people doing it full-time will probably be needed to keep up a flow of 10 new examples a month. It is expensive and every care needs to be taken to ensure that it offers good value for money.

The *Excalibur* good practice database nearly failed before it had begun because we did not know the answer to a fundamental question. Would learning providers, which were often commercial organizations in competition with one another, freely give away information that gave them the edge? Many doubted it. Clearly the conception of a bushfire, moving forward on its own, would not work unless providers not only consented to publication of their good practice examples but also to their senior staff being identified and available to others for explanation and discussion. This had to be a means for providers to help each other to achieve national goals, goals greater than themselves, happy that good ideas are a dime a dozen; it is the ability to apply them that gives a competitive edge.

The earliest providers on the database, which was then very small, were understandably nervous. Apart from anxiety that their act of altruism would not be matched by others, they were concerned that they might be inundated with phone calls and e-mails asking for advice. These were perfectly legitimate worries to which we could offer no reassurance. We all had to make a leap of faith, the ALI risking its investment in the database and the first providers their intellectual property and peace to get on with their jobs without the phone ringing every five minutes.

We can now provide that reassurance. The *Excalibur* database worked, and as the ECOTEC research showed, it worked from the start. Providers were considerate of one another in making contact but, nevertheless, new networks which were valued by everyone began to spring up. Far from hanging back from allowing the sharing of good practice, providers increasingly clamoured to be represented on the database. It was an accolade; something that said clearly to the community of adult learning providers, 'This organization is something special.' The idea of contributing a good practice example only as a direct exchange for another from elsewhere vanished very quickly, to be replaced by awareness that everybody benefits from working in a climate rich with creative ideas.

THE QUALITY CHAMPIONS PROGRAMME

One small organization, in however influential a position it might be, cannot drive forward thousands of other organizations and tens of thousands of people. To keep the wind behind the bushfire we needed to recruit hundreds more enthusiastic volunteers, lodged in the organizations we hoped would be making the progress. That was the genesis of the Quality Champions Programme. It was a unit-based set of qualifications, based on guided reflection on daily experience and validated by a distinguished awarding body, the Chartered Management Institute. Tutors were provided by the ALI. This device allowed us to secure proper recognition for the knowledge and experience acquired by people who had been providers' nominees or part-time associate inspectors or quality managers. It fulfilled a need which, given the wealth of qualifications on offer in the UK, we were surprised to find existed. Most further education colleges, for example, have active programmes of subsidized continuing professional development for their staff. Nevertheless, quality management staff from colleges joined the programme. The same could be said about other supposedly privileged employment, for example with local education authorities or the funding bodies, let alone about staff from small training organizations with little money to invest in staff development.

We held a small awards ceremony twice a year at which those receiving certificates gave a short account of their experiences. Typically, seasoned professionals would say, 'This programme has made me more conscious of what I know. With that has come greater respect from my colleagues who also now understand my contribution more clearly.'

The lesson we drew was that there are many people hidden in any national system of adult learning who usually go unnoticed, irrespective of their high value. This is probably a factor inseparable from the complexity of the arrangements for learning needed to cope with a globalized society. These people will not come forward to help the whole national enterprise progress unless they are given some positive reason to do so, but, having done so, their contribution can be immense. If better quality is your objective, then you must incentivize and celebrate the achievements of the people who bring it about and, most particularly, those people who are 'below the radar'.

MASTERS OF QUALITY ASSESSMENT

Finally, let us look at an element of the *Excalibur* programme that was close to home, a service to the ALI's independent quality assessors. Suffice it to say that appointment to a government inspectorate, at some time in mid-career when a great deal of formal qualification as well as experience is already under the belt, can be seen as the final accolade. It is a qualification in itself, superseding all others. That will no longer wash in a world that has lost its deference for appointees of the state, the British state or almost any other. While the ALI's independent assessors were extraordinarily well equipped professionally, they had to learn about inspection from scratch.

For that reason, and because of our perennial sensitivity about proving our credentials to make judgements about other organizations, we established an in-service master's degree programme with the prestigious University of Warwick. Subsequently a similar one was launched elsewhere. Recently David Sherlock chaired an advisory board overseeing the development of occupational standards for independent quality assessors in all parts of the public service.

This is work in progress. Its real potential lies not just in accrediting the skills of government inspectors but in offering a progression route from the Quality Champions Programme. It should be a feature of the *Excalibur* concept that it creates a whole, new professional workforce in quality improvement, able to carry on the techniques and philosophies described in this book, from inside adult learning organizations.

Accumulation of skills, knowledge and understanding in The Transformational Diamond, at a national and international scale, depends on a democracy of information. It implies that it is the job of organizations like the ALI to provide the seeds for a crop that may turn out very differently from anything envisaged. That crop will be tended, watered and harvested by others. In our experience, it is very difficult to create something extraordinary, to change to a culture of continuous improvement, unless that leap into the unknown is taken. We have to create circumstances in which steps towards world-class quality build up incrementally, one on top of the next, without guidance and volition from the top.

That is difficult to conceive, particularly in more didactic cultures. *Excalibur*, with the products outlined above and others, gave an example of how it might be done. It also confuted one of the sacred cows of public enterprise by showing the altruism common to both the public and the private realm.

Case Study 9

Military training: from crisis to culture change

Between 1995 and 2002, four young British Army recruits died of gunshot wounds at Deepcut Barracks in the south of England. The circumstances were suspicious. Civilian police and a Coroner's Court ruled that the deaths were suicides or of an unknown cause, a conclusion that the recruits' parents did not accept. A campaign in Parliament and the media not only created strong political pressure for wider independent inquiries, but also a growing impression in the country that the armed forces were, at best, negligent in managing the early military careers of young people.

In 2004, the ALI was commissioned by the Minister for the Armed Forces to inspect all military training establishments to make an independent judgement of whether welfare had improved since the Deepcut incidents. Controversially, this appointment was instead of a formal Public Inquiry for which the Deepcut parents and their supporters were pressing. Alongside the work of the ALI was a review of the Deepcut deaths, themselves, by an eminent lawyer and a semi-judicial inquiry by a Parliamentary Select Committee. Not only was the political and media climate very heated, but the armed forces felt themselves to be under such pressure that their willing cooperation could not be guaranteed.

The ALI carried out 24 inspections lasting about a week each. Most establishments were given notice of the arrival of inspectors but seven inspections, including at Deepcut, were unannounced. Inspectors arrived without warning and required access to every aspect of the establishment's work and records, its recruits and its staff. Recruits were able to talk to inspectors on a confidential telephone helpline. Over 4,700 recruits were interviewed by inspectors, nearly 2,200 training staff, 30 former recruits who had left the armed services prematurely, more than 230 parents face to face and another 450 through a questionnaire. Inspectors observed training establishments on a 24-hours-a-day, 7-days-a-week basis and also visited soldiers on operational duty overseas.

The ALI's conclusions were damning: that there was no reason why incidents like those at Deepcut should not happen again; that bullying and other practices forbidden by senior officers, such as punishing groups of recruits for the fault of only one, were commonplace; that welfare arrangements were well meaning but badly managed; and that firearms and ammunition were sometimes stored insecurely. While suicide rates in the armed forces were not high in comparison either with British civilians or carefully chosen international military examples, they were much higher in the Army than in the Royal Navy and the Royal Air Force. These conclusions were published in an easily readable report, *Safer Training* (2005), and given intensive media coverage.

Safer Training included specific recommendations for improvement. They were incorporated by senior military officers in a grid which allowed easy measurement and presentation of progress in putting things right. The relevant government minister took a personal interest in developments. The ALI closely monitored changes as they took place in military establishments and reported to ministers and military chiefs when improvement was inadequate or too slow. The attitude of military training staff gradually changed from one where many were sceptical and a few, hostile, to one of widespread enthusiasm and support for change. A second ALI report, *Better Training* (2007), noted 'something of a triumph of focused effort to resolve serious problems'.

This emergency action has subsequently matured into a programme and culture of continuous improvement.

Note

1   ECOTEC (2005) *Evaluation of Excalibur*, ECOTEC Research & Consultancy, December

9

Persuading

When one of the most influential British education ministers of the last century, Sir Keith Joseph, took up his job in 1981, the story goes that he was deeply frustrated. He had revolutionary new ideas by the ton, but quickly discovered he had no real power. Certainly he could negotiate and set budgets for the public education system. He could also draw up and have new laws passed through Parliament. But the schools and colleges were run by local authorities. Within curriculum guidelines defined by the demands of examinations, institutions and teachers were largely free to decide what went on in the classroom. Poor Sir Keith could have all the bright ideas in the world. The lines connecting the levers of power in his office to the places where learning actually happened were so long, went through so many intermediate authorities, that he could make all the demands he liked without much notice being taken. He could stop things but only rarely could he start them.

Things have changed somewhat in our country in the quarter century since then. Power is much more centralized. Educational instruments like a national curriculum, regular national tests for children and a national framework of awards would have gladdened the late Sir Keith's heart. But it remains the case that central government has to rely heavily on exhortation to make its presence felt at the chalk-face. Teachers, lecturers, instructors, the managers of colleges, training providers and employers offering courses to their own staff listen politely to everything the minister of the day says, but if they are unpersuaded the chances are they will hunker down and wait for the next minister and the next policy to come along.

This unwillingness among the mass of people to do anything about something about which they are quietly sceptical is pretty much universal. It is not restricted to democracies like ours, in which many take pride in being unbiddable. It happened in totalitarian countries like the old Soviet Union where a powerful streak of anarchy always lay beneath the adamantine surface. It happens in countries like Australia and Canada, where federal government arrangements must make national ministers feel sometimes that they speak to the most inattentive of audiences. Getting things done is a devil of a problem. And if, like our government, you are acutely conscious of the urgency of change to respond effectively to the challenges of globalization, but are at the same time always under pressure to steer well clear of anything that looks like overbearing authority or creating 'the nanny state', getting things done on a national scale can be a nightmare.

That is the context in which the fourth facet of The Transformational Diamond – Aspiration to excellence – has to be considered. People will not aspire to outstanding performance, strutting their stuff before a shadowy and possibly mythical global audience, unless you convince them. And to convince them you not only have to be right but you have to conjure up a future for them that is really seductive: profitable, secure and fun.

WALKING THE WALK

Before you can do any of that, you have to be in a position to be believed. Let us delicately mention the unmentionable. We have plodded the corridors of government buildings worldwide. We have plodded the corridors of organizations in the United Nations family, whose goodwill to all could scarcely be denied. Many of those buildings were run down, dirty, untidy, fully of dusty paperwork and idle people. A politician standing in front of the television cameras addressing the nation outside the real or metaphorical front door of one of these places stands no chance of convincing anyone to do anything. 'Put your own house in order before you start lecturing me!' will be the response of business and of anyone else with a fair claim to running a halfway efficient organization, private or public.

Many governments already understand this. Certainly British ministers and civil servants now occupy some almost glamorous buildings and the constant talk of public service reform gives an impression of someone at the top genuinely caring about efficiency. But ask yourself before trying the exhortation-to-excellence trick, 'Do I look credible?' If the answer is 'No' or 'Mmm, maybe', try something else. You will only make yourself look ridiculous if you tell other people to build solidly for the future while wobbling on a rickety platform yourself. Bloated, over-manned public services – let alone those that are notoriously inefficient or corrupt – make exhortation to coordinated, world-class performance from pretty much any sector of the economy sound absurd.

We were acutely aware of that when we set up our two quality assessment and improvement organizations. Everything we did, let alone what we said, was public. If we wanted to talk convincingly about aspiration to be the best, we had to run a very, very good organization ourselves. It was a practical necessity, not a matter of vanity, always to try to do something quicker than anyone else, to win more awards than anyone else. The question is always asked of judges of quality, 'Who judges you?' It is a perfectly fair question to which there have to be prompt, honest answers. One of them is to say, 'You do' and to ensure that everything possible is done to be publicly accountable. This will include not only formal reporting but also less tangible but powerful influencers like visual style.

That is the context in which we are going to spend a little while telling you how we went about setting up our last organization, the ALI, in a way that helped us build the credibility to suggest other people could do better.

If you are a private company, you have the choice of buying a prestige site and commissioning one of the world's top architects to design something wonderful for your head office. Most of the great global corporations have a trophy building that sums up its values: the HSBC Bank in Hong Kong, the Swiss Re Tower in London ('the Gherkin'), the Petronas Towers in Kuala Lumpur and so on. That option is probably closed to you if you are a public body. When the ALI was being launched we were told which city we were to be located in and, convenient and welcoming though it turned out to be, it was not the most fashionable of neighbour-hoods. It was a former manufacturing city that needed the jobs. Equally, extravagance does not sit well with a public sector ethos. We could not spend a fortune on the building. We chose a respectable modern building design, off the peg, on a business park we knew from experience would be decently maintained, but was otherwise populated with warehouses and factories. The business park location was important symbolically, as well as being a practical decision. Those were the fixed points.

It started to be possible to express our values only when we made choices about the fit-out. We selected excellent designers who were skilled in expressing ideas about working space, not just drawing attractive environments and insisting on their favourite colours. They talked to our staff. They worked out what would excite them and make them feel they were part of an organization that was special. They thrilled our home-based staff by calling them 'road warriors'; the people who had to be made instantly comfortable and welcome on those rare occasions when they visited the office. They gave shape to our conviction that we had to have a completely open space, with no offices for anybody and no special workstations, because that would express our ideas about open-ness, trust and equality without the need for words. They helped us cut wasted time by making the meeting rooms glass-walled – no sitting around shooting the breeze, invisible to the workers – and putting a small perching seat by every desk which made it easy for anyone to come and talk about an issue and make a decision, without taking more than five minutes to do it. No appointments. No e-mails to the person at the next desk. They helped us make a civilized, comfortable, efficient place to work, where people were happy to put in the hours or to take a break sitting in an armchair chatting to friends when they needed to.

The result was a runner-up award in a national competition for good practice in fit-out projects, just behind the global giant Prudential Insurance; unprecedented for a public sector organization. An intelligent modern design, on time and below budget. The result was that every visitor was bowled over by a rather beautiful workplace that was not ostentatious: it said what we wanted to say, silently but eloquently. It was a front door in front of which you could proudly stand to give out the message of excellence.

We reinforced the effect of this new approach by doing what few inspectorates routinely had done before, inviting providers to use our meeting rooms and wander freely in our offices, rather than being excluded in the interests of security. Our intention was to make it plain that the ALI was their organization just as much as ours.

Similarly, we went for every prize we could think of that would help us build the efficiency of our organization. We wanted to demonstrate it to those we needed to persuade to raise their own game. Because, as we mentioned in the last chapter, it was centrally important to us to be an exemplary employer, we worked for the UK national Investors in People award and got it in 18 months. It was a demanding thing to do in a new organization. It means that you have all the usual human resource policies and procedures in place, and can prove that everyone knows about them and uses them. It is an award that makes your organization live its ideals. If you have an equal opportunities policy but your recruitment procedure is wide open to unfair discrimination, you can forget Investors in People recognition. If your staff performance review procedure requires that twice a year you hold carefully conducted interviews with the people who report to you but, when questioned by an independent reviewer, those same people say they get nothing more than a nod in passing, forget Investors in People recognition. Having the award and continuing to hold it when reassessment comes round says something about the day-to-day behaviour, as well as the beliefs of everybody in an organization, and its official policy.

Because reports are usually unread by everybody except those who write them and those about whom they are written, and because we needed to use those reports to mobilize consumer power to help drive improvement, we entered the chief inspector's annual survey report for a national award. It won the prize as the best public information publication of the year. The judges said it was attractive, clear, unstuffy and accessible. It was reaching its audience.

Because we wanted to show that all our business practices were top class, we set about gaining the Midlands Excellence Award, a complex and really tough proposition using the European Framework for Quality Management (EFQM). It took us quite a while. With the external assessor's help we unearthed things that not only did we not do well but which we did not do at all. One of them was demonstrate local social responsibility and another was benchmarking against similar organizations. We made excuses to ourselves for not doing them. We said 'We are a national organization with most of our staff distributed country-wide.' But when we thought about it, it was important that our staff contributed voluntarily to local good causes. We said 'We are unique.' But when we thought about it, it was important that we sought out and learnt from any organization that shared some of our characteristics. And, in the end, having met all the criteria, we had the award to put on the wall. We were also able to help other companies in our region to improve and get it too. We won the added accolade of the best-run public sector organization in the largest business excellence competition in Europe, with a prize-giving in front of 1,300 business leaders. It is impossible to exaggerate the impact of such things in winning the trust and acceptance of businesses that will, at some point, have to submit their training regimes to scrutiny.

It was the same with everything we did, from our financial management to health and safety. If we did it, we wanted to do it supremely well.

There are two outcomes from that. The first one, the one we set out to achieve, was that we had a ready answer to those who challenged our right to make judgements about other people's organizations. Yes, you can always learn more and a decent humility is indispensable, but the ALI could prove that it was up with the best. It had earned the right to say what is good by being good, by knowing what is good from its own experience. But we had not bargained for the power of the second outcome, the one under our noses. If you start to win things, everyone gets the taste for it. One day the head of ICT strolls up and shows you a framed diploma announcing that *Computer Weekly* magazine has decided that the ALI is the best place in the public sector to work in ICT. Another day and up comes the head of human resources to announce that *Pay* magazine has awarded us the prize for the best-designed employee benefits package in the country. It starts to rain down good things, all of which further strengthen the organization that does the judging, the confidence and pride of the staff who work in it – and the trust of the people who are judged by it.

We have laboured the point at the risk of being thought to blow our own trumpet. Nevertheless, the point matters very much. Striving for outstanding performance is an uncomfortable business for those who do it. As well as having the potential for supreme rewards it has the potential for supreme embarrassment when you trip up. If you are going to exhort people to try it you must demonstrate a willingness to put yourself on the line first. You must have endured the embarrassments yourself and proved that your encouragement and your advice and your judgement about the degree of progress made so far are worth listening to.

DEFINING THE DESTINATION

Groucho Marx's famous quip that he would not join a club that would accept anyone like him as a member contains a profound truth. The club of outstanding learning providers you are exhorting people to try to join has to look like one worth joining. We have pounded home the point that you have to be a member yourself if you are to persuade anyone to stump up the membership fee. But how swish is the club?

Fortunately, the first part of an answer to that question lies all around us, available free. If we know nothing else in the modern world – and despite the mass of things that are meretricious, from reality TV to the notion of 'personality' – we know what quality looks and feels like. Long gone in the developed world and much of the developing world are the days when only the very rich ever came in contact with anything fine, anything excellent. Connoisseurship, the accolade of the few based on exclusively acquired taste, is no longer the arbiter of quality. The legacy of the industrial revolution worldwide is easy access to good quality at a very wide range of prices. Excellence comes in the form of an Ikea Poäng chair which will give a lifetime's elegant comfort for £55, just as do the same things – with the added benefit of transportation – in a £115,000 Bentley Continental car. We have all touched, lived with, bought something of quality.

It is not difficult to tap into that. With the ALI we worked hard to ensure that everything was consistently well designed. Our building, our websites, our publications, our staff briefcases; everything used the same set of colours, the same logo, the same typefaces. We used them to reinforce the quality message. We invited you to join in with something that you could see looked good, felt good and made its members proud. We represented high-quality learning as well as seeking to make it more widespread.

Of course, those physical characteristics had to match the more profound ethical and behavioural character of the organization. If staff wore smart badges and carried ALI-badged briefcases it would mean nothing if they were not well trained, efficient, courteous, knowledgeable. Provided that surface appearance is congruent with deeper quality, it is a supremely useful shortcut to carrying the desired message. It helps people believe you when you talk about Aspiration.

If we can accept that quality contributes to contentment, a sense of fulfilment, there will always be those sceptics who say 'Yes, but does it contribute to wealth?' In relation to education and training, that can be hard to prove. It is easy to see that people who lack sufficient education and training tend not to do well in the modern world. In our country it can certainly be proved that jobs that demand only physical labour, without trained intelligence and skill, are disappearing fast from the economy (Figure 9.1).

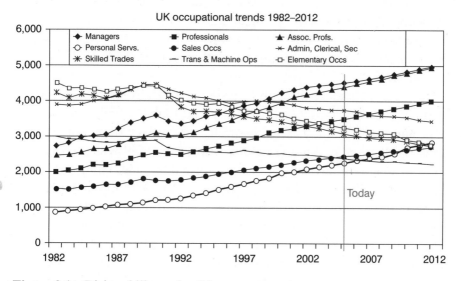

Figure 9.1   Rising skills needs of the economy
Source: DfES, Working Futures, National Report 2003–04, IER, 2004

Growth in the British economy – as we argue, the laboratory demonstrating many trends before they become widespread – is in managerial, professional and scientific jobs which demand a high level of education and training. Unskilled jobs in the British economy are falling over a couple of generations from 8 million to just 600,000. That is so clear to most British people that few are resistant to staying in some form of learning environment – including work with training – until at least the age of 18. The end of free higher education some years ago, with an increasing proportion of the costs now borne by parents and students themselves through shouldering long-term debt, appears to have done nothing to deter people from wanting to go to university. Higher education, postponing the day when they earn anything at all to the age of 21 or more for up to half of all young people, pays dividends in the long run. Lifetime earnings are higher. Job security is better for graduates. And those who are already well educated and trained get the lion's share of all subsequent learning opportunities because they are efficient learners and most quickly repay investment in them. For the individual, learning makes a lot of sense and, except among those people who for one reason or another have never experienced it to any significant extent, little persuasion is needed to make them do it. The consensus among researchers internationally is that an industry training qualification raises the lifetime earnings of an individual by 5–20 per cent, with the return from on-the-job training almost twice that from more formal learning, outside work.

However, it is more difficult to prove empirically that investment in learning has a big impact on a company's profitability or the productivity of a national economy. The research evidence is slim. Fortunately, however, there is recent and unique British research[1] which proves the value of long-term investment in work-related training. Published by the authoritative Institute of Fiscal Studies, it suggests that a 1 per cent increase in the proportion of employees trained produces about 0.6 per cent added value per hour worked and 0.3 per cent increase in hourly wages. These careful conclusions are based on 14 years of data and 85 industries. In essence they mean that the growth in productivity resulting from training is twice as large as the extra wages which have to be paid to reflect higher skills. Employers gain very substantially from training their workforce in terms of straight productivity, as well as in such important side-effects as retention. High worker turnover has significant ill-effects on productivity. And, to drive home the point that learning is not a one-off experience for the young but should be lifelong, 16–24-year-old workers are much less productive than their older peers. It is well worth investing in training the mature people already in the workforce, particularly those who have the lowest levels of existing qualifications, rather than rely on another generation of young people to bring new capabilities. The impact of training is significantly greater than additional years at school. Rather dramatically, Canadian research has found that a 1 per cent improvement in adult literacy scores, relative to the international average, produces an eventual 2.5 per cent rise in productivity.

The data we have quoted are important because they are solidly based on large, long-term samples. Nevertheless, we should also note that they *under*estimate the benefits of training in businesses and nations which are nearest the heart of the knowledge economy. The largest impact of training on productivity occurs where capital investment, research and development, and the pre-existing educational achievements of working people are also highest, for example in the typical company in ICT.

It is usually much easier to invest in training than to increase capitalization significantly, for example. More training, of higher quality, is a productivity booster available to almost every business and nation. The British government, in the *Treasury Pre-Budget Report* of 2002, set out evidence that doubling the ratio of highly skilled to low-skilled workers in a manufacturing company moved it from the bottom productivity quartile to the top. The international accountancy and research group, KPMG, showed in their *Competitive Alternatives Report* in the same year that the availability of skilled workers was the most important factor in attracting inward investment; more compelling even than labour costs, tax breaks or the proximity of markets.

There is no doubt that there is a great story to tell. Given that we can seek to persuade from a position of credibility, the message is one of punishing penalties for not investing in learning and high rewards for training adults at work. Everyone wins a lot from, in relative terms, a modest investment, provided that it is well directed. While there are clear limits on the value that training can add, the available empirical research backs up the British Treasury model (Figure 1.2) showing that training is one of the key factors in raising productivity.

This message has to be conveyed in ways that persuade learning providers and employers not just to do *something*, but to work towards being the very best: world-class. If we have authority and the message is right, what about the medium?

THE MEDIUM FOR THE MESSAGE

With the ALI we used a free monthly newspaper (also available online) to do this job. It was called *Talisman*, incorporating the letters ALI just as *Excalibur* was to do, and with a meaning that would resonate with its readers. *Talisman* is an Arabic word, meaning a magical charm bringing about extraordinary events; what could be more appropriate? In achieving motivation for learning providers to aspire to be the very best we needed effective leverage to multiply our efforts, the aim of any small organization seeking to achieve big results over matters that it does not directly control. We summarized the objectives of *Talisman* in five points:

- It would help build an identity for a learning and skills sector which was little more than a political idea when the ALI had started out in 2001.
- It would give a human face to the intimidating business of inspection, sharing our ideas and plans with learning providers as we formed them.
- It would fill the urgent need in British education and training for regular celebration of providers' successes.
- It would whisper 'quality' to its readers through good writing, good design and good paper.
- Above all, it would encourage providers not just to be good but to be outstanding.

Talisman was called 'the newspaper for adult learning' and 8,000 copies were sent to providers every month. It was printed in full colour. It contained a wide variety of material. As *Talisman* itself commented:

Talisman has had cartoons, jokes, survey reports which normally make doorstep-sized tomes boiled down to pull-out supplements or even videos (on disks attached to the page), and pictures of providers and their learners. The most reprinted issue of *Talisman* we ever published was the special on diversity. The pull-out wall chart, with its lighthearted approach to helping providers present equal opportunities promotion as a guilt-free, positive and deeply satisfying activity, is the ALI publication inspectors most often see on providers' walls.

About its usually cheerful tone, *Talisman* said:

> The whole business of helping to achieve global competitiveness for our country by raising levels of skill need not be solemn. Maybe it is inevitable that government publications should be dense and rather gloomy. But in real life, few of us achieve anything worthwhile by being unrelievedly serious. Anxiety about the state of our economy in the years to come is a poor motivator for any length of time, when the job in hand is to kindle the joy of learning in the people we all serve.

Our strong belief is that learning and skills, the realization of people's potential and ambitions, should be a cheerful business. There is a short, perilous, step between cheerfulness and inappropriate levity; the personal, organizational and national penalties for failure in the global-ized economy are severe enough that it would be wrong to ignore them. But the essence of The Transformational Diamond is to encourage people to try to do more than they think possible, secure in the knowledge that if they try and fail, help is at hand.

The publication of *Talisman* was not cheap and we considered care-fully, from time to time, whether it should continue to be free, whether its costs might be subsidized from advertising like many other 'free' publi-cations, or whether it should be sold to providers to at least meet its costs.

In our view, a decent case can be made for any one of these approaches or for the last two in combination. Organizations using The Transformational Diamond will take their own view according to their circumstances and local expectations. We decided to continue free publi-cation, without commercial advertising, because of the place of *Talisman* in The Transformational Diamond. Its power to influence, like that of *Excalibur*, described in the last chapter, came from its close association with a government inspectorate and, specifically, identifiable people in that inspectorate: Sherlock as chief inspector, Perry as director of inspection and another regular contributor to *Talisman*, and the newspaper's editor, Suzy Powling. Powling gave *Talisman* style and taste, a flair which is very unusual both in government-sponsored publications and in company newsletters. Put bluntly, publications about adult learning are too often dull, worthy and ugly whereas they should be interesting, challenging, amusing and elegant. It is a lesson well learnt in our country by such publications as *Adult Learning* and *T Magazine* but still awaiting attention in many other places.

If *Talisman*'s content and approach is compared directly with the five objectives already quoted, we get a fair summary of its style:

- It covered the many different kinds of provider in adult skills – colleges, employers, commercial training companies, local government, the police, the armed services, other countries – with equal enthusiasm, creating 'a big tent' in which similarity of aim became more important than difference of tradition or structure.
- It had a personal voice, with senior managers of the ALI and national figures able to 'think out loud' about options for future policy and even to write about deeply personal issues in a monthly *Reflections* column; *Talisman* made authority accessible.
- It always contained double-page spreads celebrating the successes of providers, particularly those that had turned their performance around using The Transformational Diamond; the competition among providers to appear in these articles became intense, with no lingering concern to cover up earlier shortcomings (see several of the case studies in this book).
- It had three designs in six years, constantly rebalancing 'look and feel', the balance between pictures and text, accessibility and bulk, to keep it at the leading edge.
- Its tone was thoughtful but relentlessly optimistic, setting successful British efforts in a global context, encouraging providers to 'think big'.

To make a shortlist of success factors for this particular approach to persuasion:

- free access;
- association with a body and people in authority;

- high production and editorial standards;
- a distinctive independent voice;
- inclusiveness and tight connection with readers;
- delight in success and understanding of failure as a valuable step on the road to success.

THE LANGUAGE OF ASPIRATION

A word or two about language. In English as used in England, education is irretrievably associated with social class. There are social hierarchies implicit in learning activities. For example, learning to think is seen as having higher status than learning to do, so that the academic study of law or pure science is regarded as more prestigious than the vocational study of business or technology. One leads to the country's elite and longest-established universities; the other to newer and less 'classy' institutions (the word is indicative). There are important exceptions. Things are changing. But if we want to hasten that change in order to overcome a handicap to global competitiveness which is a damaging relic from an earlier age, we have to take conscious steps to do so.

Britain is not alone in this. The Arab countries of the Gulf region suffer from a settled unwillingness among their indigenous populations to do manual work. The result is almost exclusive tenure of the technology sectors of their economies by expatriates, over-large public bureaucracies occupied by indigenes and private sectors mainly staffed by foreigners. In a country like Italy, with its very successful manufacturing and artisan sectors and mystifyingly complicated ways of training for the professions, traditional white collar jobs still confer more prestige than seems sensible or decent.

If we take the English of England, it is easy to find a social hierarchy in the language of learning:

High social standing

Education	University	Preparatory (private) school	Public (private) school	Student
	College	Junior (public) school	State (public) school	Pupil
Training	Training provider			Trainee
				Client (welfare to work)

Low social standing

These things are ludicrous but it would be wrong to see them as trivial or harmless. Clearly the British government does not do so because, when trying to upset the established order of things, it invents new terminology. For example, failing inner-city schools for poor people are being replaced by highly funded new 'academies', where excellent new buildings and new staff are combined to reverse long-term social exclusion with the aid of a name resonant with 'academic' associations and echoes of the dreaming spires of old academe. We share that sense that a great deal lies in a name.

For that reason we have consistently used new terminology, shorn of social connection:

'Provider'   of any organization offering opportunities for adult
               learning
'Learner'   of any adult following any form of study
'Programme'   of any kind of formal or informal learning at any level
'Teacher'   of any person involved in leading or guiding learning.

People and organizations resist. There are signs that atavistic pressures for the restoration of hierarchy are overturning the connotation-free 'learning and skills sector' with 'further education sector', for example. But the effort to use language deliberately to change attitudes is worth making and worth sustaining.

Clearly a newspaper like *Talisman* is not the only means of giving focus to persuasion and the Aspiration facet of The Transformational Diamond. Radio, television, press advertising, outdoor advertising, sponsored editorial pieces in newspapers and magazines, websites and blogs all have their places in a modern strategy for encouraging aspiration. If we had begun in 2008 instead of 2001 it is possible that we would have used something other than *Talisman*.

As things turned out, *Talisman* stood alongside the face-to-face and online media of *Excalibur* and the hands-on Assessment and Assistance of the ALI itself and its Provider Development Unit. Most, if not all, the bases were covered and there was a place for something slightly contemplative and discursive in our communications strategy that was fulfilled by *Talisman* in its newspaper format.

Also, the ALI did not work alone. Our major funding body, the Learning and Skills Council, ran a high-profile television advertising campaign promoting the involvement of employers in apprenticeship and the British government, itself, used long-term television promotion for its Skills for Life adult literacy and numeracy initiative. It is important to look around you as you choose your approach, planning and positioning to make the whole impact greater than the sum of the parts.

That is The Transformational Diamond: a coherent, planned, comprehensive set of actions, offered by one organization but conscious of the work of others and often working in partnership with them. It goes well beyond the single-purpose stereotype of most public or private sector organizations operating in improvement of learning and skills in response to the unprecedented pressures of the globalized economy. It breaks new ground and accordingly runs new risks. The test is whether or not it works better than anything that has gone before. As we shall show in the next chapter, we believe the evidence is strong that it does.

Case Study 10

Vive la différence: building enthusiasm for promoting diversity

Since 1997, the Training Standards Council and the ALI has had a specific duty to promote equality of opportunity and the celebration of cultural diversity in training for work. There are national challenges in the fact that 16 per cent of the working-age population has some form of disability and only half of them are in work, compared with 87 per cent of non-disabled people. Among the growing minority ethnic populations of Britain, unemployment is often higher than average, helping to create a disaffected and separate underclass. Gender stereotyping remains common, with unjustified assumptions about which jobs are appropriate for men or women.

These problems were widely appreciated by providers but much of the available advice left their staff feeling inadequate and guilty. They were often worried that they might be unwittingly prejudiced instead of being emboldened to resolve issues which they knew to be important in achieving both fairness and global competitiveness. Paul Drake of the Employers' Forum on Disability summed up a common misconception: 'Many organizations have policies stating that they treat all employees equally, regardless of age, ethnicity, gender, disability, sexual orientation, religion or belief. However, forward-thinking employers recognize that true equality of opportunity cannot be guaranteed by a one-size-fits-all approach to policy and practices. In order to treat employees fairly, it may be necessary to treat them differently.'

In 2005, the ALI published a special edition of *Talisman* exclusively dealing with the value of human diversity. It was reprinted twice and its centrefold was reproduced as a wall-chart and sent out to the many providers who asked for it. Demand for positive guidance was heavy and persistent.

The tone of this diversity issue was consistently positive. It included many success stories from businesses which are household names:

- HSBC Bank ensures that among its 230,000 staff, only 300 work outside their home country, symbolizing a commitment to being 'the world's local bank'; women managers in HSBC have risen from 10 per cent to 36 per cent of the total in 20 years, with a drive to achieve full parity in progress.
- The B&Q home improvement chain has a policy of employing older workers based on its experience that a new store where all the staff were over 50 achieved 18 per cent higher profits than the company average, with 39 per cent fewer absentees and employee turnover reduced by over 75 per cent.

There, too, were the results of an ALI survey showing that the clarity about diversity issues achieved through inspection and grading of the promotion of equal opportunities helped providers to improve quickly. In the one year between inspection and re-inspection, the inadequacy rates for equality of opportunity dropped sharply; from 15 per cent to 6 per cent in work-based training and from 23 per cent to 6 per cent in welfare-to-work programmes. Specific knowledge and increased confidence helped people do the right thing.

The centrefold chart showed a journey towards a world without unfair discrimination; a destination to be worked towards but perhaps never reached. It mapped four stages of sophistication, from Negativity ('You can't ram equal opportunities down people's throats') to Passivity ('Nobody gets harassed here') to Compliance and, finally, Promotion ('Diversity goes right through the business – it's not just the cherry on the cake').

The diversity issue was followed up repeatedly in Talisman with a series of 'Diversity Dilemmas', encouraging tough debate about common problems in gender, race, age and disability discrimination. The underlying message was that, in a complex society, everyone sometimes makes mistakes that upset other people. We should blame ourselves only when we are thoughtless or insensitive.

Note

1   See eg Dearden, L, Reed, H and Van Reenan, J (2005) *The Impact of Training on Productivity and Wages: Evidence from British panel data*, Institute of Fiscal Studies, London

Pells, S, Steel, D and Cox, M (2004) *Industry Training and Productivity – a literature review*, NZIER, Wellington, New Zealand

Blundell, R, Dearden, L, Meghir, C and Sianesi, B (1999) *Human Capital Investment: The returns from education and training to the individual, the firm and the economy*, Institute of Fiscal Studies, London

10

Proving it

The British government has spent nearly 30 years trying to improve workplace skills and business competitiveness across a broad front. We have seen every imaginable approach tried, every conceivable structure come and go. One useful legacy of this dizzying parade has been that almost everything we encounter across the world has some resemblance to a pattern we have come across before at home. On paper, the sophistication of our arrangements down the years has often seemed breathtaking. In practice, the problems have proved stubborn and progress has been more modest than we have often felt we deserved.

As we have described in our Introduction, very little was done to home in directly on the quality of training until the end of the 1990s. Almost nothing at all was done to improve the quality of occupational training for prisoners. Adult community education was visited by inspectors very occasionally; apparently at intervals of somewhere between 30 and 50 years.

These apparent omissions are easy to mock now. It is easy to make the criticism that the continuing education of every adult was ignored in favour of an emphasis on teaching children and preparing young people for their first jobs. That is a time-honoured preoccupation in every country. Readying the next generation to make a better fist of the world than we have made ourselves has been the aim of every parent and every government since time immemorial.

Breaking the mould, in 1998, the British government published a consultative paper exploring the potential for a new approach called 'lifelong learning'. It was called *The Learning Age*,[1] and in a foreword Secretary of State David Blunkett made a statement which still seems visionary today. He wrote:

Learning is the key to prosperity – for each of us as individuals, as well as for the nation as a whole... Learning through life will build human capital by encouraging the acquisition of knowledge and skills and emphasizing creativity and imagination. The fostering of an enquiring mind and the love of learning are essential to our future success.

Linking the ideas of lifelong learning, continuous improvement and concentration on benefit to each individual learner has proved a strategic masterstroke. We recall making visits to a number of advanced industrialized countries soon after lifelong learning took hold in Britain and being met with blank incomprehension. The older concept of once-in-a-lifetime preparation for work, at the outset, remains powerful today, bolstered by an assumption that work itself provides the necessary instruction and enlightenment to keep knowledge acquired in youth relevant. As we hope to have demonstrated in Chapter 1, the recurrent change prompted by globalization makes that proposition very unsafe even though, as a style of learning, learning-by-doing or with the help of colleagues at work is by far the preferred method of acquiring new skills for most people.[2]

However, it was perhaps another realization that brought together all the necessary factors for progress in our country around the turn of the new millennium. Demographic change, particularly in advanced economies but not only there, is the *deus ex machina* which invalidates all previous assumptions about the appropriate focus for national efforts in education and training. The birth rate in Britain and in most other developed economies has declined sharply since the 1960s. In the decade between the 1991 national census and its successor in 2001, our birth rate dropped below replacement level, from 2.4 live births per woman to just 1.6. Only now, temporarily perhaps, is it on the upswing again. The normally accepted replacement rate, the rate at which populations remain constant, is 2.1 live births per woman. If that fall in newly born Britons, combined with greater life expectancy for their parents and grandparents, is extrapolated forward to 2025, the distribution of people across the age ranges looks like Figure 10.1.

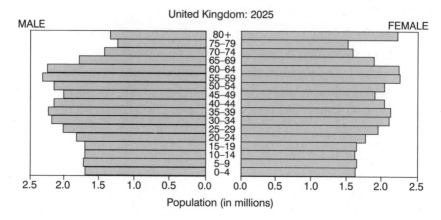

Figure 10.1   The British population in 2025
Source: US Census Bureau, International Data Base

Nineteen of the world's countries with proportionately the largest populations over the age of 65 are European. The twentieth is Japan. China's 'one child per family' policy has brought its birth rate down to 1.7 live births per woman, ensuring that it, too, will see a declining population in the coming years. As Chris Humphries, director general of the City and Guilds of London Institute, has shown in his careful analysis, birth rates in India and Africa are beginning to tumble, triggering what has been called an 'agequake'.

To be fully appreciated, the tree shape of age-range charts for most developed countries needs to be contrasted with the simple triangular distribution found in more traditional cultures like Saudi Arabia (Figure 10.2).

In the tree shape distribution, the whole of a country's economic activity depends on a relatively small fraction of the total population between the ages of about 20 and 60, with a bias towards the upper end of that

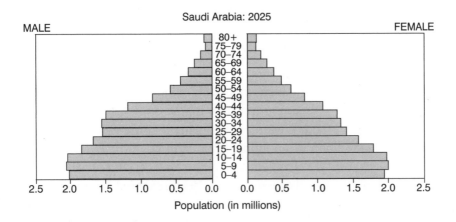

Figure 10.2   The population of Saudi Arabia in 2025
Source: US Census Bureau, International Data Base

range. A small number of successors from the indigenous population are available to replace them when they leave work for a long retirement. As Chapter 1 suggested, extending working lives, keeping women in work during their childbearing years and attracting able immigrants are vital tactics in maintaining healthy post-industrial global economies.

The upshot of all this for the UK is, as a paper from the National Institute for Adult Continuing Education showed,[3] that two-thirds of new and replacement job vacancies in the decade to 2015 must be filled by people who are already adult and already probably in the workforce. That startling illustration, so alien to our traditional assumptions about social and economic renewal by the young, profoundly changed the priority given to adult learning – and particularly adult workplace learning – by government. It was, in part, that shift which made the achievements of the ALI practicable by creating a receptive political climate and providing the necessary funding. The ALI and its predecessor the Training Standards Council cost in the region of £150 million over a decade, to which needs to be added the investment in quality improvement made by providers themselves. The scale of these investments is likely to give any government pause. However, the return is extraordinary; in Britain's case the maintenance of a place at the very top of the economic ladder and the greatest prosperity our people have ever known.

Two things need to be said at this point. The first is that, as has already been demonstrated in this book perhaps, where we described anxieties in government about the propriety of linking quality assessment and quality improvement in one organization, a traditional inspectorate is not necessarily the foundation on which one would choose to build a revolution. The ALI became something other than it was originally intended to be and, as we show in the last chapter, that made it vulnerable as well as the inventor of a new approach to improving learning.

That vulnerability was clear from the outset, and was willingly embraced in a decision that would have been regarded by many experienced inspectors as illegitimate. Rather than setting ourselves the aim of only reporting accurately what we found, good, bad or indifferent, we decided to pin our colours to a particular outcome even though it was not wholly within our control. That outcome was higher achievement among learners, with the intermediate objective of reducing rates of inadequacy among providers.

We tracked that headline indicator, the provider inadequacy rate, every quarter for six years, expressing our success or failure accordingly. It was an approach that carried a very high level of risk. We could not make providers improve. We had no powers to take the worst out of the market unless the funding agencies cooperated with us to do so. Nevertheless, it was that decision to chart our effectiveness according to one, crystal clear, measure that could be seen at a glance and appreciated by all our staff and all those working in adult learning providers that encouraged us to develop improvement services and create The Transformational Diamond (Figure 10.3).

A target, chosen well and defined carefully, is a powerful lever for change. If it is simple and related to an objective that everyone agrees is worthwhile, like benefit to learners, it can form the goal which all voluntarily pull together to achieve. It must be beyond wish-fulfilment. Unconsciously, ALI inspectors might have gradually slackened the rigour of their judgements and created the illusion of improvement to achieve their managers' wishes. However, we should have looked foolish if we had declared that providers were improving but learners' outcomes did not follow suit, and that important safeguard justified the risk of proclaiming our aim as improvement rather than only honest reporting.

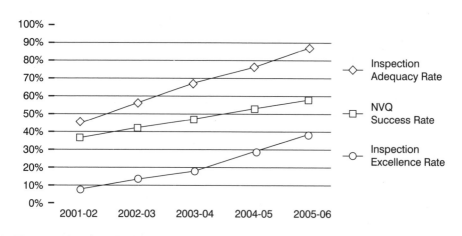

Figure 10.3   Yearly improvement of provider quality and learner achievements
Source: ALI Annual Report 2005–06

The second issue to be addressed is the concern many governments would have, that exerting so powerful a force for change on predominantly private enterprises as did the ALI and its allies would stir up a hornet's nest of unpopularity and resistance. The English learning and skills sector was and is a largely voluntarist environment. As we pointed out in our Introduction, if the ALI had failed to add value and to convince providers it was doing so, no amount of statutory authority could have prevented many of them, notably large and politically influential employers, from withdrawing from any involvement in state-led training. That would certainly have brought the whole experiment to a close.

What the ALI successfully proved was that winning consent was not incompatible with undiminished rigour in making judgements and reporting them publicly. An atmosphere of long-sustained national crisis about Britain's ability to compete successfully in the global economy helped. But most of all, it was the connection between the services that make up The Transformational Diamond – no harsh assessment without the offer of assistance; no encouragement to high aspiration without the offer of authoritative assessment of the work still to be done to achieve it; no achievement without the rewards of public celebration and consolidation of good practice – that won the support of providers for radical change.

A state agency like the ALI does not have to be unpopular and it does not have to channel unpopularity to its parent government. As the old song says, 'It's not what you do it's the way that you do it'. Openness, shared goals, civilized behaviour attract to themselves an equally open-hearted response. Figure 10.4 shows providers' views about the ALI assembled from routine (and anonymous if required) feedback from every one after its ALI independent assessment. It demonstrates a very high level of support, surely well out of the ordinary for an agency that could and did put companies that failed their learners out of business.

Just how effective was The Transformational Diamond in raising the quality of adult learning? In 2001–02, when the ALI began, nearly 60 per cent of all work-based learning providers were judged inadequate to meet the reasonable needs of learners. The government commissioned an urgent report from the Learning and Skills Development Agency (LSDA)[4] to find out why. Their research led them to put forward an important hypothesis which influenced us in developing the comprehensive approach to improvement that is The Transformational Diamond. The LSDA conclusion was this:

> Work-based learning had gradually changed from assessment of competence at work through the National Vocational Qualification in its original form, to a demanding programme of education and skill training in the workplace through the introduction of Modern Apprenticeships. This change had taken providers unawares, leaving many without the necessary capabilities to do the job. Also taken unawares were the funding bodies, which had not been able to offer the necessary support to providers to enable them to keep up, or catch up, with the changes which government required in response to the pressures of international economic competition.

At its nadir, work-based learning exhibited all the problems that can cause national provision of skills, or training in a company, to fail: unannounced changes in expectation; lack of an explicit goal to help channel energies; an absence of support and investment to ease the achievement of change; a training workforce which itself is under-trained and under-skilled. The only plausible excuse for all that is the fact that countries and companies are themselves surprised, caught unprepared, by the events around them. It happened in the UK. It happens everywhere.

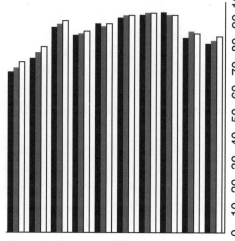

How well did the information you received from the ALI prepare you for your inspection?

How effective were staff at the ALI's national administrative centre in dealing with any queries which you had?

How appropriate was the inspection team's conduct during the inspection?

How closely did the skills and experience of the inspection team match the areas that they were inspecting?

How comprehensive was the range of evidence used by the inspection team to form their judgement?

How well was the inspection process managed by the lead inspector?

How well did the inspection team keep you informed about their emerging findings during the inspection?

How accurately does the inspection report reflect the feedback you received during the inspection?

How useful will the detailed findings be in helping you to improve the services you offer to learners?

How valuable do you think the whole inspection process will be in helping you to improve the services you offer to learners?

0 10 20 30 40 50 60 70 80 90 100

■ 2003-04   ■ 2004-05   □ 2005-06

Figure 10.4 How providers rated the ALI's performance (%)

Source: ALI Annual Report and Accounts 2005–06

In that year of 2001–02, only 24 providers out of 480 which were assessed by the ALI, 5 per cent, achieved good or outstanding grades (grades 1 and 2) for everything they did. Four of them were military training establishments, nine specialized in engineering and well over half were employers training their own staff in small numbers, rather than specialist training organizations specifically contributing to the national stock of skilled people.

At the other end of the quality scale, 80 providers were inadequate in everything they did. Among them, only one in ten was an employer training its own staff but one-third were specialist training companies, and nearly half were located in the areas of industrial decline in the north of England; the place of greatest need. More than half of all providers had poor leadership and management, contributing substantially to a total of inadequate provision which appalled us and appalled government.

The achievement levels of learners were, if anything, even worse. In the very best area of learning, engineering, 59 per cent of apprentices achieved their qualification but in the worst, hospitality and catering, only 16 per cent – one in six – did so. The average proportion that succeeded was around one in three. Imagine any circumstance where you are twice as likely to fail as to succeed and you will understand the shock these statistics caused and the readiness of government to consider original, previously untried, methods to fix the problem.

A year later the fix, the quickly evolving Transformational Diamond, had helped bring the overall inadequacy rate down from 60 per cent to 46 per cent. By 2003–04 it was down again to 34 per cent and the first impact of this marked improvement in providers' skills was seen in a rise of 6 percentage points in learners' average achievement rates. That delay is to be expected, as better teaching feeds through into better end-of-programme results a year or two later.

By 2003–04, 78 providers achieved consistently high grades out of the 470 assessed by the ALI; 17 per cent of the total or more than three times the proportion two years before. There were still 47 consistently bad providers, compared with 80 two years before.

Two years on again, in 2005–06, the provider inadequacy rate was 12 per cent, only one-fifth of what it had been in 2001–02. Instead of the 24 good providers of that year, in 2005–06 the ALI found 151: six times as many. Twenty-four providers were poor, fewer than one-third as many as in 2001–02. While apprentices' achievement rates continued to lag behind improvements in teaching, they had risen to nearly 60 per cent on average and by 13 percentage points in the last year, showing their acceleration.

The extent and pace of this improvement is unprecedented and unmatched in our country. Those providers that worked enthusiastically alongside us in the ALI did spectacularly well. Those that stood aside and persisted in poor performance lost their contracts for government-sponsored training in a savage cull of around 250 organizations.

These statistics obviously sketch a change from gloom to joy, from failure to success, from victim to winner for many thousands of people in learning organizations, and especially for learners themselves. But what of the impact on the country as a whole? Government statistics published in 2007 give an indication:

- There are 440,000 fewer children living in workless households since 1997, assisted by the provision of 1.3 million more childcare places.
- There has been an increase in Modern Apprenticeship annual starts from 75,000 in 1997 to 250,000 now.
- There are 600,000 more businesses in the UK than in 1997.
- The UK has halved the gap in productivity with France, closed it completely with Germany and kept pace with the rate of improvement in the United States.
- The UK has the highest rate of investment in its economy from overseas of any country in Europe.
- British science is rated second only to the United States worldwide in terms of citations.
- One million more adults are now qualified to level 2 and 1.7 million basic literacy and numeracy qualifications have been achieved since 2001.

Obviously, our work has not been material to all of that. However, it has been a significant part of the creation of a new, challenging but optimistic climate in adult learning for work, which permeates the British economy.

Probably the most complete expression of this, and of the success of our methods in bringing adult learning for work into the government policy mainstream, is *Prosperity for All in the Global Economy – World-class Skills*; the Leitch Report. Lord Leitch, reporting to the UK Treasury, concluded that even allowing for the progress made in the past decade Britain will 'have managed only to run to stand still' by 2020. He said: 'On our current trajectory, the UK's comparative position will not have improved significantly. In the meantime, the world will have continued to change and the global environment will be even harsher.'

Even though the UK has enjoyed 14 years of unbroken economic growth, the highest employment rate in the G7 with two million new jobs created since 1997, and a significantly improved skills base over the last decade, Leitch still believed that 'The scale of the challenge is daunting.' Adopting the goal which the ALI chose in 2001, to become 'world-class', Leitch set a series of targets to extend the achievements which were made using The Transformational Diamond still further:

- functional adult literacy and numeracy up from 85 per cent and 79 per cent respectively to 95 per cent;
- level 2 qualifications up from 69 per cent of adults to 90 per cent;
- 1.9 million more level 3 (technician level) qualifications by 2020;
- a further doubling of the number of apprenticeships to 500,000;
- degree-level (level 4) qualifications up from 29 per cent of adults to 40 per cent or more;
- productivity up by a further 15 per cent;
- employment growth rate up by 10 per cent.

Lord Leitch's focus was on adult skills because, as he said, re-expressing the conclusion of the National Institute of Adult Continuing Education, '70 per cent of the 2020 working age population has already left school'.

Whether we look at statistics or the passage of adult learning to the centre ground of public policy, it is clear that The Transformational Diamond – in combination with other strategies and agencies – has delivered very marked results. For Britain and the ALI, the moment was right in the year 2000 for a surge in the development of economically valuable skills and of government policy to support them. Implementing Lord Leitch's recommendations will extend and renew the momentum at least until 2020. In the world of democratic politics, concentration on one issue, however important, for 20 years is close to eternal life.

For British organizations that have yet to join in, or still more critically for other countries that stand hesitating on the brink of the sometimes difficult changes needed to flourish in the global market, the magnitude of what they will have to achieve expands with every passing day. That prospect really is daunting.

In our last chapter, we show how it is possible to gain benefit from The Transformational Diamond, starting from wherever you happen to be today. It is all too easy to dismiss or delay admitting a need for change. We have given a candid account of the very serious weaknesses our country had to overcome and it is possible that, elsewhere, people will say 'The Brits really lost it. How stupid was that!' We can only say that this kind of dismissal is likely to provide cold comfort. Our experience is that almost every country, developing or developed, has a skills deficit. Sometimes people believe they can ignore it because extraordinary wealth in raw materials papers over the cracks of an underproductive population. Without wishing to be melodramatic, we need to point out how quickly things can change and go wrong. Britain went from the 'swinging sixties' to the economic collapse of 1979's 'winter of discontent' in the blink of an eye, our underlying faults brutally exposed by the oil-price crisis earlier that decade. It can happen to anybody, any company, any country. What we are offering, at the very least, is a means to check that the factors for continuing success in adult learning are clearly visible and kept in balance with other priorities in public education and training.

Case Study 11

A fair cop: enriching the learning of police constables

Britain's police force was among the world's earliest. It has a proud history of crime solution, crime prevention and community service. It is essentially local, relying for its effectiveness on building the support and cooperation of ordinary citizens. For that reason, the independence of separate county forces is jealously guarded for most purposes. Achieving radical changes in training consistently across the country and without temporarily reducing the quality of recruits is difficult.

Entrants to the police all begin at the most junior rank of constable. Their initial training was standardized through delivery of a 15-week formal residential course at a regional centre, with a further six weeks during the first two years of employment. Learning the ropes through patrolling their local streets under the supervision of a senior constable provided the practical element of what was, in essence, an apprenticeship.

The ministry responsible for policing, the Home Office, decided to replace this established scheme with a new programme for 'student officers'. It is based on a precisely defined national occupational standard, organized in 22 units of study with performance competencies. Much more of the initial training is carried out on the job, with a wider range of experiences built in than was gained through neighbourhood patrolling. This includes not only many aspects of policing but also attachment to voluntary welfare organizations such as drug-awareness centres, women's refuges and care homes for older people. The presence of young police constables among groups of vulnerable people not only sensitizes them to social problems but is also an investment in the future consent of communities in policing. However, achieving consistency across the country and over time is made more difficult by closer engagement with the complexities of today's society.

The solution was in commissioning the ALI to monitor and evaluate a pilot for the programme. No student police officer would slip through the net of a new and untried training scheme. The inevitable teething troubles in a new programme would be spotted, analysed and resolved before the scheme was extended nationwide in 2006. Five police forces volunteered to run the pilot under the supervision of the ALI. They included the largest in the country, the Metropolitan (London) Police, and a range of others from both the cities and the countryside.

The ALI's usual approach was applied, helping to ensure comparability in the quality of training with that provided for civilians. ALI influence was also evident in a shift in emphasis among the senior police officers and government officials managing the programmes, from policies and procedures towards the experience of the individual constable. A Home Office official commented: 'The ALI brought impartial authority to the evaluation process – they were independent of the Home Office and the (police) service. They are experts in the field of adult learning and brought rigour to this process. Their methodology puts the learner at the heart of the evaluation as opposed to the structures and processes.' This focus on the quality of the learning, on the outcomes of the programme rather than its form, also helped to secure the enthusiastic support of officers immediately involved with the hurly-burly of modern policing and anxious that newcomers should be fully prepared for it. A sergeant said: 'The ALI assessors were very approachable and put you at your ease during the interviews. They were very flexible in moving around the force area to meet as many members of the (programme) team, tutors and supervisors as possible.'

In developing advanced training schemes, involving a complex set of experiences, it pays to build in quality assurance and continuous improvement at the design stage, before full national or large company-wide adoption. This is now standard practice with British government schemes, including many that are at risk because of their versatility and responsiveness to changing workforce demands among employers. It reduces the risk of adaptation to the forces of globalization.

Notes

1   TSO (1998) *The Learning Age*, The Stationery Office, London
2   ACE (2007) *Practice Makes Perfect*, Annual survey of learning at work: National Institute for Adult Continuing Education (NIACE), UK
3   ACE (2005) *Eight in Ten: Adult learners in further education*, National Institute for Adult Continuing Education, UK
4   LSDA (2002) *Making the Grade*, Learning and Skills Development Agency, London

11

Adapting the model

While we were writing this book, discussion with colleagues on the far side of the world threw up an issue we have encountered before. 'We like what you have achieved', they said, 'but we do not like the idea of government inspection and our teachers would not stand for being observed while they taught.' The temptation on these occasions might be to reply that the reservations protect everyone but the learner and it is unlikely that one can achieve the end without willing the means.

The extraordinary effectiveness of The Transformational Diamond certainly lies in the fact that it always offers the information or the encouragement or the support an organization needs to make progress once it has determined on doing so. But what our friends were saying was only that they found some aspects of the Assessment facet of the Diamond unpalatable. That should not stop them from gaining benefit from the model, albeit partial. We rest content in the private conviction that, sooner or later, an organization that has been successfully motivated to become world-class (Aspiration) is going to ask how good it is now, how much work it has to do to reach its new goal and of what kind (Assessment). The Transformational Diamond works because it addresses universal needs in learning and because, to a large extent, each facet reflects an understanding that people have to reach for themselves.

Let us tease out for you how different applications, different interpretations, might work in practice, starting in our own backyard.

We developed The Transformational Diamond on the basis of our experience of running two British government inspectorates. One had power to inspect as a condition of contract, the other in law. It was a criminal offence to impede ALI inspectors in the reasonable conduct of their duties, including by denying them access to business premises or to records and the computers on which they were stored. The ALI never used these powers of coercion and would have regarded it as a serious failure if it had. As we have tried to show in this book, the essence of quality improvement is willing consent, trust and a wide groundswell of enthusiasm. None of these thrives under duress.

In just a few months during 2007, the whole political context we had worked in and where we had done our learning about quality improvement changed. A new prime minister from the same political party succeeded Tony Blair after 10 years in power. His political emphasis was on demonstrating not only that a change in leadership had taken place, but also a change of substance. His initial policy emphasis was on reshaping the structures of government, conscious that the proportion of people qualified to vote who actually did so fell at election after election. The considerable power of central government departments had proved disappointing in bringing about real benefit to citizens, however well conceived were their policies and however generously financed their initiatives. Even a parliamentary democracy as solidly established as that of the UK and a politician as gifted as Blair had been unable to ride the wave of globalization in a way that kept the whole population on board. Public services were still not seen as good enough to match expectations and costs. The gap between rich and poor was rising, in Britain as in most other developed economies, just as wealth poured in as a result of success in global markets. Where there had been failures, they had often seemed more the fault of the shape of national governance than of any lack of good intentions and ability on the part of those in government.

This is a conclusion with extraordinarily far-reaching consequences. In the past few decades we have had a Department for Education and Science; a Department for Education and Employment; and, most recently, a Department for Education and Skills. Plainly, none of these configurations had worked to the entire satisfaction of the government of the day, in matching the demands of learning to the globalized economy. From a structure of ministries based on functions and budgetary silos, with imperfect connection between them, England is edging towards one that is organized more thematically. Instead of the vertically integrated

Department for Education and Skills, with its all-through, cradle-to-grave responsibilities, we have a new ministry concerned with every aspect of childhood: schooling, welfare, safety, justice and health. Alongside, for adult learning, we have a ministry concerned with innovation for the globalized economy: science, universities, colleges and workplace skills.

Neither can act alone. As children grow into adulthood, so does responsibility blend gradually from one ministry to another. It is the technique of pipelining used to achieve desirable policy outcomes more effectively on a large and infinitely complex scale.

Complementing these horizontally integrated, policy-focused ministries, we have single-issue advisory commissions of experts and narrowly defined operational agencies. The trick of making organizational matrices of this kind work is to reduce the number of components on each axis of the matrix to a practicable minimum. Our ALI has merged with the former schools inspectorate, Ofsted, to form a new Office for Standards in Education, Children's Services and Skills, with responsibilities spanning both new ministries – and several others. This new inspectorate will apply a lighter touch to providers, leaving those that have proved capable in the past 14 years much to their own devices and concentrating regulatory functions on the poorer performers. Quality improvement services developed by the ALI, which we have described in this book, are now lodged in a new Quality Improvement Agency which, rather than offer them itself, commissions them from private and charitable consultancies. The facets of The Transformational Diamond are scattered over the matrix. Without doubt more rearrangement and reorganization is to come.

Let us summarize for you the key services on each facet of The Transformational Diamond:

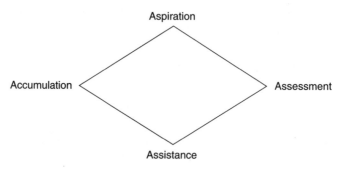

Aspiration
- Demonstrable authority to make sound judgements
- Encouragement to excel rather than comply
- Celebration of providers' successes
- Approachability and down-to-earth optimism
- Giving expression to a 'club' everyone wants to join

Assessment
- Easily accessible published framework
- Widely acceptable criteria for judging quality
- Regular self-assessment involving everyone concerned
- Authoritative verification by independent expert assessment
- Publication of unequivocal judgements
- Follow-up to assure correction of weaknesses
- Fairness guaranteed by an open approach to complaints

Assistance
- Incremental and developmental approach to follow-up assessment
- Free but conditional availability of direct help for 'weak-but-willing' providers
- Deployment of 'soft' information arising from assessment
- Engagement at the system level as well as that of the individual provider
- Clear distinction between assistance and assessment

Accumulation
- Creation of an autonomous quality community
- Presentation of validated examples of good practice
- Recognition for contributors to a stock of high-quality provision
- Practical help to deliver high-quality learning
- Public celebration of successes

For us, these things were embodied to a large extent in *Talisman*, the ALI itself, the Provider Development Unit and *Excalibur*, respectively. They were closely connected philosophically and organizationally and therefore infused, we hoped, with a common humanity and cheerful determination to succeed. We know this works spectacularly well in securing continuous improvement for the benefit of individual learners, employers and the nation alike. How can we ensure that its most significant instruments of change shift seamlessly into a new environment?

Governments do what governments will, everywhere in the world. The stability of policy varies dramatically, from the countries of continental Europe where education and training systems are recognizably based on those devised 200 years ago by Napoleon, to the UK and its former colonies which are more prone to try winning the game by pushing over the chessboard every few years. In every organization, every region and every country, we have to deal with the changing circumstances with which we are faced. There is no single pattern which, if copied faithfully, will deliver success in training adults to succeed in a global economy for ever and a day. Adopt. Adapt. Learn. Evolve. Innovate. These descriptions of change are the constants of the globalized world, not the exceptions. What every learner, every chief executive in every business, every minister in every government has to do is to find the means for continuous progress that lie beneath them. Those means will vary from place to place, from time to time and from circumstance to circumstance. In this final chapter we aim to illustrate some approaches in the full knowledge that everyone using The Transformational Diamond will have to find its optimum expression for themselves.

A NEW PATTERN IN ENGLAND

Our underlying purpose in the past 14 years has been to endow providers of learning with greater skills, greater confidence and higher ambition to devote to the service of adult learners. We, and those many other people working towards the same end, have succeeded to a large degree. As we come to terms with a rewriting of the state infrastructure, the strongpoint from which we can begin to reshape the system of adult learning appropriately is the maturity of those providers. David Sherlock's last annual report as chief inspector of adult learning for England, in the autumn of 2006, ended by saying, 'It is for them to make the best of their inheritance.'

What might a provider-centred system look like, if it conformed to The Transformational Diamond? Can we also use the Diamond to identify any gaps?

The most sensitive issues are concerned with Assessment. Self-assessment is well established and the framework that guides it is willingly accepted. As we suggested earlier in this book, there are indications that the reliability of self-assessment is not yet sufficient to give the necessary guarantee of good service to learners. The probability is that the role of self-assessment up until now, predominantly as a means of accountability to government funding agencies and inspectorates, has compromised the accuracy of the result. By influencing all but the very boldest providers to shun the lowest grade, grade 4, it has made them inflate their performance above the threshold by about one grade point. What is needed in the new circumstances is to reaffirm the role of self-assessment as a means of providing accountability directly to learners. We suggested earlier that this might be done by publishing summaries of self-assessment reports annually, including self-awarded grades, with any awarded by independent assessors alongside for comparison. That should help to restore the honesty of the process and to underline its central purpose in the quality management of providers. The question remains, will this be enough?

The competence with which self-assessments are carried out can always be improved and, as we write, an extensive programme of government-funded workshops is being launched to achieve this.

The crunch will come in securing independent verification of self-assessment. The continuation of the ALI service by Ofsted will provide this to some extent, but 'a light touch' implies concentration on the diminishing band of weak providers. Those that are capable will receive less attention and the impact of Ofsted independent grades on the probity of self-assessment grading will inevitably become less powerful over time. Less intrusive and less comprehensive government inspection has a cost, in terms of the gradual attrition of objective information about details of the operation of providers.

In trying to supplement the remaining oversight by inspectors, two main choices present themselves: peer review by largely informal groupings of providers assessing one another; or peer review strengthened by a core of expert assessors, rather in the manner of the Quality Assurance Agency (QAA) for higher education in our country and the accrediting associations of the United States of America.

It might be argued that the latter option differs only slightly from a government inspectorate consisting of relatively few well-trained expert assessors aided by a large number of associates from providers or the consultancy industry. These associates are, in most cases, 'peers' of the people they help inspect. However, the decisive difference is one of ownership. QAA is the property of the British universities, and the accrediting associations that of the American universities and colleges. This difference is enough to persuade us that it offers the more reliable approach to independent assessment, in combination with the necessary transfer of responsibility to providers. It has the additional virtue that it could be organized nationally in a country the size of England, preventing the emergence of local or regional differences of judgement which might well result from peer review by a cluster of providers united mainly by their proximity or their familiarity with one another.

There are those who would argue that growing trust in the expertise of providers should be marked by the removal of all independent assessment. It should suffice that providers carry out self-assessment regularly and publish the results. This is an attractive prospect because of its simplicity. However, we think it unlikely to reassure those who are responsible for the very large sums of public funds involved or, indeed, employers[1] paying similar amounts of private money. It is excessively vulnerable to gradual loss of contact with reality, given the lack of a genuine market in much of adult learning, already mentioned. Even more decisive, for us, is the absence, in a wholly internal scheme, of opportunities for assistance when things go wrong or for broadly based accumulation of knowledge and experience. If everyone marches alone, isolated, the synergies of The Transformational Diamond cannot apply.

With some reservations, then, there seems no reason why the Assessment facet of the Diamond cannot work effectively in the new circumstances. There will be tensions between a desire to rely on a universal scheme of self-assessment and peer-based review, and the more gradualist approach of 'earned autonomy', implicit in 'light touch' inspection. We incline towards caution, offering provider-based arrangements only to a proven elite group in the first instance. This is much as British universities began, with a separation between those that were long established and validated their own awards, and those that worked with a national council that awarded degrees. A step-by-step progression offers fewer opportunities for – possibly terminal – setbacks. Nevertheless, judgements will have to be made about the political appetite for gradualism and its acceptability among influential providers.

The three other facets of the Diamond offer different challenges to those who want to maintain and adapt them.

Let us consider Assistance. The significant factors here are the availability of a reliable judgement that a provider is inadequate and why it is inadequate; a decision that market forces will not suffice to offer a remedy or replacement; the resources to support intervention; the expertise to intervene effectively; and a means to check independently that performance has improved and continues to improve. Provided that the funding agencies remain locally represented to the extent that they are able to make sensitive judgements about whether or not it is in the public interest for a failing provider to survive, there is no reason why this facet of the Diamond should change materially.

The inspectorate, Ofsted, or the peer review body would make a judgement of inadequacy; the appropriate funding agency would decide to intervene or not; the Quality Improvement Agency or its successor would offer the money and the approved consultants to help the provider. The process would be less seamless, more complicated by additional agencies in play, than once it was. Those difficulties could be ameliorated, at least, by using the type of formal three-way contract for improvement introduced by the ALI Provider Development Unit. If required, the Assistance model continues to work in substance, accommodating the necessary changes of detail.

Going on to Accumulation, under the new English arrangements, the formation of quality communities to develop and carry forward a body of shared experience and memory continues to rest mainly with providers. In our country there are several groupings and associations that have important roles to play in this. Some, like the 157 Group of large, high-quality colleges, have the potential to pioneer a new infrastructure by developing their own national accrediting associations to attest not only the quality of member institutions but also qualifications for learners. In this respect they might come to resemble, for example, the vocational institutes of New South Wales in Australia, causing TVET to approach much more nearly the structures and power of higher education. Whether or not this kind of model is adaptable to privately owned, competing, learning providers, probably operating through their association, remains to be seen. It would be deeply unfortunate if the unity of purpose forged in the learning and skills sector among providers in different forms of ownership were to be broken into a host of mutually hostile splinter groups.

A database of good practice could readily be made available by groupings of this kind: examples would be selected through the accreditation process and published on a website carrying the prestige of the group. Alternatively, as it is at present, the *Excalibur* database could continue with examples identified by Ofsted and disseminated by the Quality Improvement Agency, although 'light touch' inspection, bypassing excellent providers to a large extent, might soon put the best practice beyond view.

There are, in this, organizational options, differences both marked and subtle, that allow our model to be adapted to meet different pressures and serve well in different environments.

Only when we come to the encouragement of Aspiration do we meet any real dilemmas. The strength of the ALI in this arena was that it had all the necessary tools to hand. It was close to government but not as close as to be regarded as alien by providers. It had extraordinarily intimate access to providers and the most detailed understanding of their strengths, weaknesses and potentialities. It could force the unwilling to try harder, as well as coax and encourage the goodwill that existed more widely. It had the means to communicate regularly and persuasively.

These things are not so readily available to either the new government departments or the funding bodies. Who will champion aspiration most effectively is not yet clear but championed it must be. The Diamond helps us spot the gap.

The UK system is moving in the broad direction of liberalization. After a period of strong central direction to tackle shortcomings identified by the government, advantage is being taken of the additional capacity of providers, developed under the guidance of state agencies like the ALI, to run the system on a looser rein. The ambition is clear: to release a further surge of creativity among providers by giving them even greater liberty to experiment, to expand at home and overseas, and to explore wider limits of responsibility. The strains in the system are likely to be between this welcome sharpening of responsibility for excellence and a continuing need to regulate, to audit, to assure consistency which remains in the realm of various government agencies.

Let us take as an example one of the three rings in our model of English TVET (Figure 1.4), that containing the means to develop employer-validated occupational standards and transferable qualifications. In our new arrangements employers, colleges and training providers will be able to seek national recognition for awards they, themselves, make to recognize attainment in programmes they devise and offer. Vendor qualifications, like those offered by Microsoft and Sun Systems, among others, should find a place in the national qualifications and credit framework. This will be beneficial in that the great mass of economically productive learning which is today invisible to government, unaccounted for in the statistics describing the availability of workplace skills in Britain, will show itself for the first time. Difficulties will emerge perhaps as each constraint representing the national interest is applied: by skills councils imposing national strategies and the broad requirements of employers; by the Qualifications and Curriculum Authority underlining the need to maintain national standards and a close fit with a national transferability framework. These abrasions will be necessary to maintain the virtues of the present system while bringing more of the submerged mass of the iceberg of work-related training to the surface.

UPRATING AN ORGANIZATION

If the Diamond helps us understand and accommodate radical change at the national level, how might it assist a large, widely dispersed organization? We have in mind a national company offering blended learning, which has to adapt to meet the changed operational environment, as well as to gain competitive advantage from its own growing maturity. Like several others in our country, this organization has over 500 local learning centres, owned and run by about half that number of colleges, private providers and charities which, in effect, provide services on a franchise.

If external control exercised by the state is to be loosened, the duties of quality management to be fulfilled by the company will become more onerous. Controls have to be more effective in order to protect the values of the franchising company's brand; to guarantee consistently good service for learners; to reveal good practice which can be shared, powering the continuous improvement of the whole organization; and to produce an accurate account of quality through self-assessment which will satisfy a light touch inspection and the demands of funding bodies so that revenue keeps flowing. One reasonable response to this is to conclude that more effective control is synonymous with tighter control. In effect, as the state relaxed its grip on local learning centres, the franchising company would take its place by tightening up. There are plenty of means of doing so, including the use of compliance-based standards like those in the ISO 9000 series.

However, greater centralized control of this kind carries a cost. Performance requirements have to be tightly specified, reducing the scope locally to produce something outstandingly good just as effectively as they do something lax and unacceptable. Tight specification tends to restrict outcomes to the middle ground because that is what can be foreseen. Compliance with these requirements has to be policed, usually by staff employed specifically for the purpose. The analogy might be with old-fashioned manufacturing, in which a host of inspectors approved or rejected products at the very end of the line. This is an expensive solution which runs the risk of souring relationships between head office and the people who deliver services on its behalf. It is a high-overhead, low-trust, middling-performance model which is unlikely to produce the dynamic and flexible learning suited to the global economy.

If, however, we consider the same set of circumstances and results which are desirable in the light of The Transformational Diamond, the picture changes. Instead of investing in tighter performance specifications and controls, we start out instead by defining the values of the franchising company and building consensus and enthusiasm around them. We begin with shared Aspiration. Our investment is then directed towards fostering honest, expert self-assessment, through training franchisees; building trust to enable people to be candid, to experiment and sometimes to fail; and completing an accurate approach to Assessment by positively exploiting the dispersed locations and diverse ownership in the business to create a strong peer-review process. To return to our manufacturing analogy, workers on the production line themselves take responsibility for the quality of what they make, rendering the white-coated inspector and his box of rejects obsolete.

Assistance, again, can be a matter of peer support guided and organized from the centre. Accumulation might use the peer-review process to identify good practice, disseminated and celebrated through excellent internal communications.

There is, in this approach, scope for innovation and for the development of a business culture which is self-policing, based on adherence to shared beliefs and values and the incentive of recognition by professional peers. This kind of outcome is the goal of every modern manager.

A DIFFERENT CULTURE

In 2007 we produced a study of TVET in Saudi Arabia.[2] As we showed in the last chapter, the Kingdom of Saudi Arabia has a very high birth rate. In the past 30 years its population has trebled and is still growing at an annual rate of 4 per cent. Sixty per cent of these people are under the age of 21 and 100,000 young Saudis enter the job market every year. However, a quarter of the country's population consists of non-nationals, mainly from the Indian subcontinent, the Philippines and Indonesia. Foreign labour, skilled and unskilled, holds 95 per cent of the jobs in the private sector. Saudi nationals hold 90 per cent of the jobs in the public sector, mostly white-collar administrative positions. The government labour minister commented in 2006 that 'Saudis prefer to have comfortable jobs, having less hours and ensuring job security'. Unemployment among Saudi men is very high at, perhaps, 25 per cent. This pattern of employment, combined with population growth so high that even in boom times for oil prices *per capita* income is falling, is a time bomb capable of overwhelming the country's political stability.

The Kingdom depends heavily on the export of oil and gas. It is a command economy, highly centralized under the direction of an absolute monarchy. It has been decided that the only way out of the bind in which the country finds itself is to overcome the reluctance of young Saudis to train for technical jobs in the private sector, over time displacing expatriates. In principle, given the high concentration of authority, this should not be too hard. There are 37 technical colleges serving perhaps four million young people. But these colleges, with some notable exceptions, bear the marks of centralized control: standard buildings, equipment and curriculum, regardless of local job opportunities, and tenured staff with little authority to innovate.

Saudi Arabia has decided to open 90 new colleges and 160 new technical institutes to help resolve its extreme problems. Does The Transformational Diamond help determine how best they might operate?

The key to the problems faced by the Kingdom is bringing about a change in Aspiration. Unless many, many more young men can be persuaded to embrace a career which requires practical skill and some degree of manual work, unless religious and cultural traditions can evolve to allow more women into the workforce, it is unlikely that the country will achieve a soft landing. At some point it is likely to succumb to the combination of internal pressures, regional instability and globalization. The stakes are very high.

The proposed solution in this case is that the new colleges and institutes should be run under contract by a variety of overseas countries. Aspiration, in other words, is to be provided through the successful example of other economies, other attitudes to technical training and to work. An existing and very successful example is the Saudi Japanese Automotive Higher Institute near Jeddah, where Japanese industrial working disciplines and practices in continuous workforce development attract many more applicants than can be accommodated. This may not be an ideal means of encouraging aspiration. It is certainly one that carries the real danger of a backlash against alien innovation, but it shows promise of working in this very unusual environment.

Assessment is likely to be a matter of government monitoring of contract compliance, aided by advisers from oversees. The development of occupational standards with the advice of two British awarding bodies illustrates the approach that might be adopted. Again, this is not an ideal expression of the Diamond, but it is likely to form the basis of a sound start from which something more local can be built. Family and tribal allegiances make it unlikely in the short term that independent assessment could work successfully as a wholly Saudi operation. Independence has to be bought from abroad in this case.

Assistance will be a matter for contractors themselves. It is unlikely to figure prominently in an initiative so dependent on competitive contracting. A vital component, Accumulation, will consist of Saudi staff working alongside expatriate teachers and managers in the new colleges, learning from them until they are ready to take over. This practice is working well in the Saudi Japanese Institute, with Japanese advisers heading a hierarchy of foreign and Saudi senior instructors and Saudi junior instructors, many of whom already are graduates of the institute. Accumulation will in the first instance consist of a kind of apostolic succession among generations of the best TVET staff. In time, means will need to be found to energize and refresh the system of new colleges from within and across the board using the kind of technique for encouraging and sharing good practice which is described in this book.

The Saudi example shows how the Diamond can be used to identify issues and to assign lines of development. In this case it would form a sensible basis for drawing up a long-term development plan, moving from high dependency on foreign TVET suppliers to increasing independence – Saudiization is the preferred term – and the growth of a system which is more capable of self-revitalization than are the existing technical colleges. For this benign progress to take place a wide range of social and political hurdles have to be surmounted. No easy matter. For the moment, however, Saudi Arabia can build on the two assets it has, money and a willingness to learn from others, and The Transformational Diamond can be used to mark out clearly what it needs to do, year by year, to achieve its ultimate objective.

REFLECTION

The examples that might be explored to show how our methods can be used productively are endless. We have watched, fascinated, the launch of a government TVET inspectorate in Thailand, where success in the global market is pivotal but the exercise of critical judgement culturally disagreeable. It was accomplished by the inspectors simply visiting colleges and giving kindly advice in the first instance. For a second cycle of visits, grading against a framework based on the English *Common Inspection Framework* is in prospect. This might be described as Assessment masquerading as the encouragement of Aspiration, until colleges start to ask 'How good am I?' Rome was not built in a day. Having laid the first stone it becomes increasingly easy to lay the rest.

As we write, we have in prospect a range of projects which seem likely to prove once again that the model is sound, that it provides a way into the most obscure and apparently intractable of problems. Ultimately, its strength is that it assumes the best in people. It assumes that ordinary people invariably can do extraordinary things if the goals and the tasks to be accomplished are properly understood and methodically addressed.

Our conviction that this is true comes not only from a decade or more of guiding change in that most obstinate of organisms, the democratic nation state, but from earlier careers teaching talented adults and running institutions of learning. The first step towards supreme achievement is to want it. The second is to understand what has to be done to attain it. The third is to rest easy in the confidence that failure can always be redeemed and will, in the end, be a source of greater accomplishment. The fourth is the confirmation which is achieved from reflecting on success, analysing it and sharing it with others. To teach is to learn. Learning is both universal and timeless.

What has changed in the fairly recent past is the degree of urgency around learning. In some ways this is a matter for regret. It reflects a world in which the young cannot play their way into adulthood and adults cannot rest, allowing what they learnt in youth to gently mature. The globalized world is noisy, demanding and obsessively busy. At its worst, it is materialistic to an extent that dehumanizes and diminishes us. But it has, perhaps for the first time in human history, a counterbalancing potential to remove whole populations from poverty. That is a goal worth striving towards, even if we have to ride a tiger to get there.

Our hope is that this book will offer some security of understanding and a sense of direction. Stay clear of jaws and claws and hold tight.

Case Study 12

Jamie Oliver and *Fifteen*: learning changes lives

International chef Jamie Oliver sprang into the limelight at the age of just 22 with his own television series, *The Naked Chef*. Well grounded by his own happy childhood in the family pub and restaurant and a thorough training at Westminster College and the famous River Café, Oliver has concentrated as much on social projects as on his successful media career, books and cooking.

In 2001, he launched a charitable foundation to help 'unemployable' young people into successful careers through apprenticeship at his restaurant, *Fifteen*. Each year now, applications for the *Fifteen* project are narrowed down to a shortlist of 120 16–24-year-olds, some homeless, some with criminal records and some drug and alcohol abusers. Further selections are made through interviews, tests for aptitude in cooking and a two-day outdoor adventure camp, until the final 15 or 20 candidates are chosen. Oliver said of the 2006 intake:

'This year, we got all the parents and students in on the first day to tell everyone exactly what they go through, what things we've seen in their child emotionally and mentally, how they will change, how they'll get better, and there wasn't a single father there. Only having one parent around is one of the biggest causes of these kids' problems.'

The programme starts with a week-long induction, an initial three-month training period at catering college and a month's work-experience in a restaurant. After that the trainees go to work in a *Fifteen* restaurant, now branched out internationally from the first in London's East End. *Fifteen* is pitched at a fine-food clientele, challenging trainees to attain not only top culinary quality but also outstanding customer care. Oliver emphasizes the special place of the hospitality industry in giving people a first step into rewarding careers: 'The lovely thing about cooking is you don't have to do economics or maths or spelling to do well. All you need is the ability to listen, smile, be a pleasure to be around and work like a dog.'

Oliver's trainees often need help with life-skills like managing the money they start to earn: 'We have a close relationship with Barclays Bank, which trains our kids to look after their cash and manage their own accounts. Probably one of the biggest social problems in the country is the lack of that ability – people spend far more than they have.'

The *Fifteen* foundation not only teaches skills in a tough but increasingly high-profile industry, but an appreciation of good things. Oliver says that 'our ability to rehabilitate kids depends on excellence. I don't simply want to teach kids to cook. We teach kids to grow.'

Jamie Oliver used the transformational power of learning and well-managed media exposure to air a national problem in 2005 with another pioneering television series, *Jamie's School Dinners*. He taught school cooks to prepare healthier food than the 'chips with everything' usually on offer. As a direct result, extra government funding of £280 million was given to the school meals service, raising the amount available for a primary school child's lunch from 37p a day to 50p. Oliver is still only 32.

Source: Adapted from *Director* magazine.

Notes

1   The CBI estimates that British employers devote over £30 billion a year to training their staff, a figure which, if adjusted to offer a like-for-like comparison, is probably similar in scale to public funding for adult learning.

2   ALI (2007) *New Skills for Saudi Arabia: A review of provision for improving workskills*, ALI and The British Council, UK.

Index

NB: page numbers in *italic* indicate figures

accessibility   146–47
accumulation   141, 144, 151, 193
  and accessibility   146–47
  and concentration   146–47
  of corporate memory   146–47
  under new English arrangements   197
  and validity   146
adapting the model   190–206 *see also*
    case studies; Transformational
    Diamond
  in a different culture   201–03 *see also*
      Saudi Arabia
  in England   194–99
  reflection   203–04
  updating an organization   199–200
added value, measuring   50–53
Adult Continuing Education, National
    Institute for   179
adult guidance   59–60
Adult Learning   170
adult learning   48–49, 176
  and focus on skills   185
  health benefits of   48
Adult Learning Inspectorate (ALI)   4–6,
    64–65, 71–72, 127–31, 88–89, 103,
    124–25, 127–31, 139–41, *142*,
    142–50, 155, 179–82, *182*, 183–86,
    193, 195
  and *Excalibur* 6 *see also main entry*
  Assessment and Assistance   172
  criterion of benefit to learner   72
  face-to-face teaching   150
  grades comparisons   88
  instructional materials   147–50
  Learner-centred Self-assessment   46
  overseas   6
  Provider Development Unit   6,
      128–31, 172, 197 *see also main
      entry*
  quality improvement doctrine   72–73
  training of inspectors   80
apprenticeship(s)   57–58, 173
  Advanced   57
  and Land Rover   77
  Modern   57–58, 182–83
  NVQ   57, 99–100, 182
aspiration   159, 171–73, 193 *see also*
    Saudi Arabia
  and dilemmas   198
  encouragement of   198
  shared   200
assessment   31, *31*, 90–91, *91*, 123, 125,
    151, 193, 194, 196, 202 *see also* self-
    assessment

and confirming progress   126–27
and reassessments   125–26
Assessment and Assistance, connection
      between   129, 131, 134
assessment frameworks   32–34 *see also*
      Quality Assessment Framework
      reasons for   32
assistance   193, 196–97, 200, 202
Australia   14, 24, 197
      and skills standards   23
awards   49, 162

building a national quality movement
      (and)   139–57 *see also*
      accumulation; Adult Learning
      Inspectorate (ALI); case studies;
      corporate universities *and Excalibur*
Quality Champions programme   154
masters of quality assessment   155–56

case studies
      building a national quality movement:
            military training   156–57
      consequences: Cheadle Royal Industries
            135–37
      consequences: learning and skills in
            prisons   137–38
      data: Toni & Guy   120–22
      enriching learning of police constables
            187–88
      feedback: judging learning   86–87
      globalization: Unipart plc: an exemplary
            learning organization   26–27, 49,
            67
      learning changes lives: Jamie Oliver and
            Fifteen   204–05
      persuasion: *vive la différence*   173–75
      proving it: a fair cop   187–88
      self-assessment: JHP training   104–06
      standards and frameworks: BMW
            Group UK Ltd   43–45
      using the framework: West Berkshire
            Audit Community Learning
            64–65

challenges of globalization *see*
      globalization
change, necessity for   9–10
Chartered Management Institute   154
China   11, 19, 24
      birth rate in   178
City and Guilds of London Institute   23,
      178
Collins, J   61, 62
Common Inspection Framework   48,
      203
Competitive Alternatives Report (KPMG,
      2002)   167
concentration   144–45, 146–47, 151
confidentiality   84
consequences   123–38 *see also*
      assessment; case studies *and*
      observation/observers
      driving home change   124–26
      and Provider Development Unit
            128–35
      and result of PDU assistance
            133–35
corporate memory   146–47
corporate universities   139–41 *see also*
      Excalibur
      and Unipart   141
culture change   124

data (and)   98–100, 107–22
      apprenticeship example   117–20
      community (on death)   69–70
      comparisons (and)   114–17
            areas of learning   115
            cohort progression analysis   116–17
      focus on outcome   113–14
      management   120
      misleading perceptions   108–10
      numerical measurement and questions
            111–13
      presentation of   110–11
definition(s) of
      good learning   53
      quality in learning provision   34–35

demographic change   177
  birth rates   177–78
  populations   177–78, *178, 179,* 179
diversity
  promoting   173–75
  value of   55

Economic Co-operation and Development,
  Organization for (OECD)   2
Economic Horror, The   10
ECOTEC research and evaluation
  143–44, 147, 149, 153
Employee Development and Assistance
  Programme (EDAP) (Ford)   49
England, a new pattern in   194–99 *see
  also* United Kingdom (UK)
Entry to Employment (E2E)   57
equal opportunities legislation and gender
  policies   56
European Framework for Quality
  Management (EFQM)   30, 162–63
European Union   15
Excalibur   141, *142,* 142–47, 150–53,
  155–56, 172, 193
  and concentration   144–45, 146
  and ECOTEC   143–44, 147, 149, 153
  effectiveness of   143–46
  elements of   142–43
  good practice database   151–53, 197
  and staff involvement   145

feedback
  from observation   82–85
  good practice in   125
figures
  assessment, components of   *91*
  English education system performance
    68
  Excalibur (ALI)   *142*
  how providers rated ALI's performance
    (%)   *182*
  knowledge economy, shock of *13*
  Learner's Journey   *47*
  observation form *81*

population (British) in 2025   *178*
population (Saudi Arabia) in 2026   *179*
productivity and growth: five key
  drivers   *15*
productivity gap   *17*
provider quality and learner
  achievement, yearly improvement
  of   *181*
rising skill needs of the economy *165*
Transformational Diamond *31*
TVET model *21*
Forrester, V   10
Framework for Excellence   104
France   12, 13, 15
Fresh Start, A   68
Further Education Funding Council
  (FEFC)   2, 3, 4, 5

global market   49, 140
global trade   14–15
  as continental or regional   15
  and mercantilism   14–15
  and tariff barriers   14
globalization   8–28, 128, 179, 204 *see
  also* case studies; knowledge
  economy *and* United Kingdom (UK)
  national skills strategies   19–20
  and recurrent change   177
  references   28
  skills and productivity   15, *15,* 16–17,
    17, 18
  technical and vocational education and
    training (TVET)   20–26 *see also
    main entry*
  and the UK: the British experience
    11–15

information and communication
  technology (ICT)   115–16, 128
inspections   2–6 *see also* judging
  learning *and* observation/observers
  deferral of   71
  light touch   197–98
  of military installations   71

preparation for   71–74
  of prisons   71
instructional materials   147–50

judging learning   67–68, *68*, 69–87 *see
    also* case studies *and*
    observation/observers
  confidentiality   84
  feedback   82–87
  good learning *see* quality in learning
    provision
  inspections   71–74 *see also main
    entry*

Klein, N   10
knowledge economy   12–15
  and the UK   12, *13*, 13–14

leadership, assessing   61–62
Learner's Journey   46, *47*, 48, 62, 100,
    111–14
learning *see also* case studies *and* judging
    learning
  adult   48–49, 64–65
  areas of   115
  effective   53–54, 68
  good *see* quality in learning
    provision
  investment in   166
  and matching to learners   56–59
  pattern in   80, 82
  provision   34–35
  responsiveness vs quality   64–65
  support for   59–60
  work-based   58, 77–78, 88, 109–10,
    182–83
Learning Age, The   177
Learning and Skills Council
    172–73
Learning and Skills Development Agency
    (LSDA): report and research
    182–83
Legrain, P   10–11, 14, 28
  and mercantilism   14

Leitch report: *Prosperity for All in the
    Global Economy – World-class Skills*
    185
  and targets   185–86

management skills   61–62
Moser, C   68, 87

National Vocational Qualification (NVQ)
    3
No Logo   10
notes and references   28, 66, 87, 106,
    157, 175, 189, 206

observation/observers   69–82
  as self-assessment process   70
  credibility of   78–80, *81*, 82
  feedback from   82–87
  and monitoring visits   127–28
  of teaching and learning   73–74
  training in/of   73–74
Office for Standards in Education (Ofsted)
    2–3, 103, 195, 197

parity of esteem   16
peer evaluation   42–43, 70
peer observation schemes   79
Perry, N   93–94, 115
persuasion (and)   158–75 *see also* case
    studies
  credibility   159–64
    and office design   160–62
    and national awards   162
  language of aspiration   171–73
  new terminology   172
  quality   164–65, *165*, 166–68
  Talisman   168–71 *see also main entry*
Powling, S   170
prison
  inspections   71
  learning and skills in   137–38
  occupational training in   178
productivity and growth   15, *15*, 16–18
progress, confirming   126

Provider Development Unit (ALI)
128–35, 193, 197
Assistance deal 131–32
and other providers 129–34
and restriction on assistance 132

qualifications, value of 48–50
Qualifications and Curriculum Authority
(QCA) 23–24
quality assessment 69, 155–56
and improvement 6, 24–25
Quality Assessment Framework 35–43,
46, 48, 49–50, 53–54, 64, 96–97, 125
see also using the Framework
(for/and)
and evidence/judgements 39–42
'why?' question 42–43
Quality Assurance Agency for Higher
Education (QAA) 2, 195
Quality Champions Programme 154
Quality Improvement Agency 197
quality in learning provision 75–78
benefits and shortcomings of 34
definition of 34–35
quality management 119

Raising the Standard 148
references see notes and references

Saudi Arabia 10, 178, 179
aspiration, assessment and assistance in
201–02
and skills standards 23
and TVET study 201–03
Scotland
and Scottish Qualifications Authority
(SQA) 24
and TVET 20
self-assessment 71, 88–106, 126,
194–95 see also case studies
and accountability 92
data 98–100 see also data (and)
evidence for 96–98
features of 92–93

honesty in 99
and independent assessment 90–91,
91
independent verification of 195
leadership and achievement of 95–98
and organizational culture 102–04
over-complexity in 93–94
and regulation 91–92
units for 100–01
Silent Takeover, The 10
sitting by Nelly 85
skills strategies, national 19–20
staff satisfaction survey (MORI) 102–03
Standard Occupational Code 4
standards and frameworks 29–45 see
also assessment frameworks and case
studies
good learning: quality in learning
provision 34–35
Quality Assessment Framework
35–43 see also main entry
SWOT analysis 133

Talisman 5, 108, 168–71, 172
objectives of 168
style of 170
tariff barriers 14
teachers/teaching 67–78 see also
inspections and judging learning
evaluating 71, 75–76
ineffective 70
professionalism of 69
shortcomings of 76
technical and vocational education and
training (TVET) 20, 21, 21–26, 31,
32, 54, 69, 80, 88, 197, 198 see also
standards and
frameworks
assessment frameworks 30, 32–34 see
also main entry
awarding bodies for 23–24
in other countries 23
occupational standards for 23
providers of 20–22

qualifications and standards for   23
quality assessment and improvement
        24–25 *see also* quality assessment
and Sector Skills Councils   23
and verification   22
Training Standards Council   3, 4–5, 103,
        111, 115, 124, 179
Transformational Diamond   31, *31*, 70,
        73, 90, 123, 128, 131, 135, 141, 144,
        155, 159, 169, 170, 180–82, 184,
        185–86, 190, 194, 196, 198, 199–203
        see also accumulation *and* assessment
and aspiration   159, 172–73
effectiveness of   182
key services on facets of   192–93
trust   22, 90
TVET *see* technical and vocational
        education and training (TVET)

United Kingdom (UK)   11–12, *13*,
        13–15, *15*, 16, 31, 102–03, 128,
        194–99
apprenticeships   57
disability benefits   14
economy of   166, 185–86
effective learning in   68, *68*, 69
ethnic minority communities in   55
government statistics (2007)   184–85
and immigrants in unskilled jobs   14
Investors in People award   162
language of learning   171–72
liberalization of system in   198

Midlands Excellence Award   162
and parity of esteem   16
school qualifications   51
and self-assessment   88, 90
traditional inspections   5–6, 32
Treasury Pre-Budget Report (2002)
        167
welfare-to-work programmes   114
workplace skills in   199
United States of America (USA)   12, 13,
        15, 17, 18, 195
and productivity   18
and tariff barriers   14
using the Framework (for/and)   46–66
        see also case studies; leadership;
        learning *and* Learner's Journey
added value, measuring   50–53
equality and diversity   55–56
grading   63–64
qualifications, value of   48–50

validity   146, 151
value-added measure (VA)   52

welfare-to-work programmes   114
Jobcentreplus   114
New Deal   114, 140
work-based learning/training   58, 77–78,
        88, 109–10, 182–83
Workstep   128, 130, 134

Yemen   8–9